NEW YORK

- A in the text denotes a highly recommended sight
- A complete A–Z of practical information starts on p.115
- Extensive mapping throughout: on cover flaps and in text

Printed in Switzerland by Weber SA, Bienne.

1st edition (1995/1996)

Although we make every effort to ensure the accuracy of the information in this guide, changes do occur. If you have any new information, suggestions or corrections to contribute, we would like to hear from you. Please write to Berlitz Publishing at one of the above addresses.

Text:	Don Allan, Martine Lamunière
Editors:	Delphine Verroest, Olivier and Isabelle Fleuraud
Photography:	Jon Davison
Layout:	Cristina Silva
Cartography:	Visual Image; New York subway map © NYCTA, used with permission. A current subway map may be obtained at any subway token booth.
Thanks to:	The New York Convention and Visitors Bureau, Donald Olson and Steigenberger Reservations Services for their help in the preparation of this guide.
Cover photograph:	*New York City skyline, with the Hudson River in the foreground* © Tony Stone Images

CONTENTS

New York and the New Yorkers

Face it: New York is the greatest. Coming in from the airport or down a highway, that first sight of Manhattan's skyscraping profile injects a shot of adrenaline that lets excitement loose in your bloodstream. You just know that something special is about to happen.

Excitement mounts as you leave your hotel and are swept along in the high-energy currents of the crowds. What do you crave? Views and scary thrills from the top of a tower? Laughter and tears in the latest hit show? World championship sports? A foot-long hot dog, or a gastronomic tour of international cuisines? A classical concert every night? The treasures of five continents in priceless museum collections? Glamorous boutiques (BARGAINS! SALES!) and glitzy showbiz hotels?

Wall Street, Broadway, Madison Avenue, Fifth Avenue –

Manhattan's street names are international symbols. Day and night, the pulse of these arteries throbs ceaselessly in your ears. As traffic stalls, blocked energy escapes in harsh, piercing hoots and loud siren wails. Lights flash brief commands: 'WALK', 'DON'T WALK', 'EAT', or 'BUY'. Whatever they urge, the basic Manhattan message is 'Do it NOW!'

This somewhat bewildering first impression soon recedes. The simple east-west, uptown-downtown orientation of the grid of streets and avenues is quickly mastered. Soon, you discover that the great city is a fascinating collection of quite individualistic neighbourhoods, each marked by history, distinctive architecture, commercial specialization or ethnic identity. In the middle is a miracle of grass, rocks, ponds and old trees, a vast space open to the sky – Central Park. Nature in New York simply has to be the greatest, too: the park is twice the size of Monaco.

New York isn't the capital of the USA, but with the United Nations here it claims to be **5** the capital of the *world*. Visitors from just about anywhere will find countrymen clustered somewhere among the 7½ million inhabitants. Indeed, some 40 percent are foreign-born or the children of immigrants; one in four New Yorkers is black; about one in five is of Hispanic origin. All this is reflected in the faces, names and customs of New York. It's a major point of entry where many immigrants stay and swiftly become 'reggela Noo Yawkuhs' in the fast-forward Babylon that manages, somehow, to be simultaneously the most American and least typical of all US cities. As Frank Sinatra sang, 'If you can make it here, you can make it anywhere ...'

Some 5½ million foreign tourists a year add colour and the sound of their accents to the scene. In recent years New York has done a lot to attract visitors and to clean up its reputation as crime-ridden, dilapidated, bankrupt and rude. It has its seamy side, to be sure, but it is now safer, cleaner and more caring for the needs of tourists than it was for many decades.

In preparation for the 1992 Democratic Party Convention the city went all out, refurbishing monuments and hotels, putting 300 percent more cops on the street, persuading many top restaurants to offer fixed-price lunches for $19.92 and scheduling free concerts and

*C*entral Park is a permanent stage for hardworking freelance performers and artists.

6

other events all over town. The effort was a big success. Many improvements, such as the set lunches, have become fixtures. Branches of several banks now change foreign money, a basic amenity hard to find not long ago. The transit system now has a hot line that gives subway and bus information in dozens of languages. Even the subway cars have shed their ugly graffiti, thanks to a Japanese no-stick scrubbable metal.

New York is the greatest because of its prodigious capacity for regeneration: something new is always surfacing. Entire new neighbourhoods and attractions appear, like Battery

New York in Figures

The five boroughs (Manhattan, Brooklyn, Queens, the Bronx and Staten Island) have a total population of seven and a half million. With the surrounding suburbs, this figure rises to about 12 million and, if the outlying satellite cities are included, the total attains a phenomenal 16 million inhabitants.

New York City covers an area of some 322 square miles (834sq km). It has 6,400 miles (10,300km) of streets and 18 miles (29km) of beaches. There are 1,100 parks, squares and playgrounds with a total area of 37,000 acres (15,000ha); at least 100 museums and 400 galleries; more than 30 department stores; 400 theatres; about 100 skyscrapers; 3,500 churches; 15,000 restaurants; 100,000 first-class hotel rooms and 12,000 taxis.

About four million people ride the subway every day. Some 2½ million catch a bus. The number of shops is well up in the thousands. Roughly 17 million people visit New York each year, 5½ million of them from overseas.

Another amazing fact is that in New York there are more Italians than in Venice, more Irish than in Dublin and more Jews than in any other city in the world.

Park City, built on landfill from the World Trade Center site, or the South Street Seaport complex of ships, shops and eateries. The Times Square area, once given up for lost to sleazy hustling, displays some smashing new hotels. It is the hub of expanding tourist bus operations by day and shines brighter than ever at night under its spectacular flashing ads.

As one district goes down, others rise. So if Fifth Avenue south of Rockefeller Center seems in decline, given over to dubious discount emporia and sidewalk vendors, the trendy galleries and restaurants of So-Ho and TriBeCa are blooming with beautiful people in an area that not so long ago was deserted after dark. The Guggenheim Museum has opened a SoHo modern art branch.

Chinatown is a living city within the city, steadily swelling from legal and clandestine immigration and spilling over into the Lower East Side. The area claims the largest Chinese population outside Asia. Uptown, Koreans have revolutionized the eating habits of apartment-dwellers with their ubiquitous, colourful all-night fruit stands and salad bars. Indians have replaced elderly Jews in operating the city's news-stands and there is now a growing 'Little India' district to the north of Gramercy Park. 'Little Italy' is shrinking a bit, but nearby Greenwich Village bursts at the seams, especially at weekends, when the record shops, bookstores, movie theatres and bistros are jammed with youthful crowds. While the East Village retains lively vestiges of the Hippie 1960s era, mixed with elderly Ukrainians clinging to their traditional turf, across town in the West Village, the gay quarter is approaching historical landmark status alongside genuinely venerable leafy streets with mellow Georgian façades.

A melting pot it isn't, but New York lets all these contrasting elements coexist with

Queen of skyscrapers, the Chrysler Building looks down at the distant borough of Queens.

8

remarkable tolerance. They all unite in cursing the taxes, the weather, New Jersey drivers and the ineptitude of their National League baseball clowns, the 'Mets'. (The 'Yankees' in the American League are still the team of legends Babe Ruth and Joe DiMaggio, too heavy with history for levity.) It's okay for New Yorkers to bad-mouth their town, but they'll turn in unison on any stranger who dares to criticize. After all, they'll demand, isn't it the greatest? Where else can you watch ten zillion lights go on at dusk from the towering spire where King Kong met his end? Where else can you drink green beer on St Patrick's Day? Or hear opera and theatre free under the stars? Where else can you get the jump on fashion in the places where trends are launched?

The list of things that make New York exciting and unique is almost endless, as any New Yorker will tell you. If you don't believe them, then go and see for yourself!

A Brief History

A Florentine in the service of France, Giovanni da Verrazzano, discovered the bay that would one day become the site of the most powerful city in the world. He landed on Staten Island in 1524, just 32 years after Christopher Columbus's first voyage to America. Today a bridge bearing his name (but spelt with one 'z') stretches elegantly across New York Bay.

Verrazzano received a good welcome from the Manhattans, a local tribe of Indians who guided his ship to a safe landing. Although he wrote an enthusiastic report of his visit to the French king, François I, a century passed before any settlers actually came to live on the estuary.

New Amsterdam

In 1609 an Englishman called Henry Hudson was sent to look for a westward route to the Indies. He didn't find what he was after, but he sailed up the broad river (which was later named after him) and discovered the beautiful Hudson River Valley. Returning to Holland with quantities of furs, fruit and tobacco, Hudson stirred up a great deal of interest. In 1621, the Dutch West India Company was granted the charter to trade, plant colonies and defend its outposts in North and South America.

The first settlers arrived under the company's auspices in 1624, and the following spring built a small town on the southern end of Manhattan Island, calling it New Amsterdam. An idea of its size may be gained at what is now Wall Street (see p.41), where a Dutch wooden palisade then marked the village boundary.

For 40 years the Dutch remained in possession of the island of Manhattan, purchased from the Indians for the legendary sum of $24 in beads and cloth. Under the leadership of two governors, Peter Minuit and Peter Stuyvesant, the town took on a Dutch look, yet from the beginning it was the most cosmopolitan centre in the New World. The earliest immigrants

HISTORICAL LANDMARKS

1524	Verrazzano discovers New York Harbor.
1626	Peter Minuit buys Manhattan Island from Indians for $24.
1664	English seize New Amsterdam and rename it New York.
1789	Washington inaugurated first president on Federal Hall steps. NY population stands at 33,080 (in 1790).
1812	City Hall opens; British blockade harbour.
1858	Olmstead and Vaux design Central Park; Macy's opens.
1882	Thomas Edison's first urban electric lighting plant opens.
1883	Opening of Brooklyn Bridge.
1886	Statue of Liberty unveiled by President Cleveland.
1898	Population of the five boroughs is over five million.
1904	The first subway opens, with a five-cent fare.
1913	The Woolworth Building opens, the first 'skyscraper'.
1920s	Clandestine speakeasies serving liquor spread over the city, flouting Prohibition.
1927	Lindbergh flies from Long Island to Paris.
1929	Stock market crashes, setting off the Great Depression.
1930-31	Chrysler and Empire State Buildings constructed, Rockefeller Center begun.
1939	New York World's Fair opens. War closes it in 1940.
1952	UN headquarters complex completed.
1962-66	Lincoln Center performing arts complex constructed.
1965	Malcolm X assassinated in Upper Manhattan.
1970	World Trade Center completed (bombed 1993).
1977	Stock Market crash.
1990	Democrat David Dinkins becomes NY's first black mayor.
1993	Republican Rudolph Giuliani becomes mayor of NY.

included Walloons, Scandinavians, Germans, Britons, Spaniards and Portuguese Jews, not to mention black slaves from the Caribbean. In 1643 a priest counted 18 languages spoken in this town of 1,500 inhabitants. Other settlements had developed outside Manhattan in what is now the Bronx area, in Brooklyn and in the Flushing area of Queens.

Life was by no means easy, though. In those days of poor communications, it was practically impossible to do anything without prior approval from the home country, which took ages. Relations with the Indians were tense and the climate was harsh. What's more, the British – who held all the colonies around New York – were knocking at the door.

Unable or unwilling to put up a fight, the Dutch settlers surrendered to an English fleet on 8 September 1664. King Charles II gave the colony to his brother, the Duke of York, and New Amsterdam was rechristened New York. In the 18th century the town grew into a city of 25,000 and life became more comfortable. A city hall and several churches were built, and New York saw the foundation of King's College (today's Columbia University), as well as the creation of its first newspaper. During this period, many traders were able to make their fortunes.

However, the people were increasingly irked by British control. New York, like the other colonies, was split between 'loyalists' to the Crown and 'patriots' who favoured independence. On 27 June 1775, half the town went to cheer Washington as he left to take command of the Continental Army in Boston, while the other half were down at the harbour giving a rousing welcome to the English governor, who had just returned from London. Similarly, the New York delegates voted against an early version of the Declaration of Independence. A few days later, however, when the final text had been drafted, they agreed to sign it. Even in those days, New Yorkers were already a people apart from their fellow countrymen.

The New Republic

New York remained a British stronghold throughout the war and only gave up after final surrender in Virginia in 1781. Two years later England recognized the independence of the American colonies. Washington returned triumphantly to New York and bade farewell to his officers at Frances Tavern (see p.42). (see p.42) New York City was briefly the first capital of the new country and Washington took the oath of office as its first president on the balcony of Federal Hall, overlooking Wall Street.

In the early 19th century, the City of New York was much richer culturally than any other

*S*oHo façades and the World Trade Center twin towers typify Manhattan's heady mix of old and new.

13

American city. The political capital had moved to Philadelphia in 1790, but New York developed as America's shipping and commercial centre.

In 1800 the population grew to 60,000 – twice what it had been ten years earlier. Already the city had problems that persist today: housing shortages, too few policemen and firemen, not enough water and inadequate public transportation facilities. Diseases and epidemics were frequent, sometimes even forcing people to 'escape' to Greenwich Village for the duration of the summer.

In 1811 the state legislature came to the conclusion that any further growth of New York must be regulated. A special commission proposed that all new streets should henceforth cross each other at right angles, with streets running east–west and avenues north–south. Only Broadway (see p.27), an already established road leading to the north, was exempted. The plan was immediately adopted, with the result that everything above 14th **14** Street is now a grid.

Burgeoning Town

When the Erie Canal linking the Great Lakes to the Hudson River opened in 1825, New York became the ocean gateway for an immense hinterland. Business flourished and shipyards abounded in this major port, but even so there was too little work for the majority of newcomers. Blacks, Irish and German immigrants lived on top of each other in crowded shanty towns. The Catholic Irish were resented, and religious conflicts erupted.

In December 1835, a terrible fire destroyed the heart of the business district, including almost all that remained from the Dutch era. However, the city recovered with amazing celerity. Old neighbourhoods were soon rebuilt and the city began to expand northward.

In 1853 the Crystal Palace of the first American World's Fair went up near the site of the present New York Public Library, and five years later work started on Central Park and St Patrick's Cathedral. In spite of the new prosperity, this was also a very turbulent period for New York: between 1840 and 1860 the city's population rose from 300,000 to 800,000, and riots, street fights and demonstrations were not uncommon.

Following the outbreak of the Civil War in 1862, the town's growth came to a temporary standstill. New Yorkers were markedly unenthusiastic about the Union cause, and the draft law – providing for a $300 exemption fee that only the rich could afford – met with ferocious opposition from the foreign-born working class.

After the war the boom continued unabated to the end of the century, giving rise to unprecedented corruption on a large scale and to wild property speculation. Financiers Jay Gould and Jim Fisk attempted to corner the gold market, but ruined half of Wall Street on 'Black Friday' in September 1869. Boss Tweed of the Tammany Hall political organization ran New York with his cohorts and managed to fleece the city of some $200 million.

The construction of railways opening up the western lands, expansion of mines and mills, and development of the new petroleum industry and the automobile were all financed by New York banks.

Great fortunes were made by the Vanderbilts, Harrimans, Morgans, Carnegies, Rockefellers and Fricks, among others. These tycoons amassed the fabulous art collections and funded many of the philanthropic and cultural institutions that make New York what it is today, from the Metropolitan Museum and Opera to Rockefeller Center and the land that the family made available as a site for the United Nations.

Mass Immigration

During the second half of the 19th century influxes of immigrants flooded into New York in search of a new and better life. The potato famine in Ireland and revolutionary ferment in Central Europe had brought in Irish and Germans, who were soon followed by Italians, Poles and Hungarians. The first important wave of Jews fleeing the pogroms of Russia **15** and Eastern Europe arrived in the 1880s. Over two million newcomers landed in the city between 1885 and 1895, welcomed (after 1886) by the recently inaugurated Statue of Liberty (see p.90). For the first time Congress decided to impose limits on immigration, banning the Chinese, the sick, madmen and anarchists.

Adequate housing for the constantly expanding working population was an important problem: a subsidized housing programme was launched but could hardly begin to deal with the desperate situation.

The new middle class moved to West Side neighbourhoods near Central Park, while the comfortable brownstone houses and mansions of the rich spread up Fifth Avenue and on the East Side. In 1870, construction started on a bridge to connect New York with Brooklyn, a sizeable town in its own right. The invention of the elevator by Elisha Otis made it possible to put up 'skyscrapers' eight or ten storeys high.

In 1898, New York (from then on known as Manhattan), Brooklyn, Queens, the Bronx and Staten Island amalgamated into Greater New York with a population of more than three million. The early years of the 20th century witnessed the first genuine skyscrapers: the Flatiron Building (1902)

Behind classical Washington Square arch lies unconventional Greenwich Village.

reached the impressive height of 286ft (87m) with 21 floors. In 1904 the first subway line opened. Lively Greenwich Village, which became a centre for artists, writers and theatre people, acquired a bohemian reputation. Following World War I, the exclusive shops and more fashionable department stores moved to Fifth Avenue above 34th Street, and New York began to experience traffic jams for the first time.

In October 1929 the business boom burst with the catastrophic crash of the stock market. Breadlines and jobless apple sellers became a common sight, and a shanty town sprang up in Central Park.

In 1934 a dynamic Italian-born mayor named Fiorello La Guardia fought to introduce an important number of public welfare measures and civic reform. He rebuilt much of the Lower East Side, but not, unfortunately, once-fashionable Harlem, which became the overpopulated home of not only the blacks but also the Puerto Ricans who arrived in a new wave of immigration.

World City

When the United Nations set up its headquarters in New York after World War II (see p.32), the town started calling itself 'World City' – an apt title. Ever since the first settlers disembarked here, New York has been most cosmopolitan. Neighbourhoods change abruptly with a casual crossing of streets; dialects, languages, costumes and cuisines abound in endless variety. Foreign-language papers are published here as each community tries to retain its individuality. Almost every ethnic group has its own special holiday and parade along Fifth Avenue.

New arrivals keep coming all the time: Koreans with their grocery stores, Haitian cab drivers, Indians controlling the news-stands, Central American domestic workers, Vietnamese and Thai restaurant hopefuls. For the newcomers, as for the previous generations who have enriched New York with their cultures, the lure is the same: New York remains a symbol of economic opportunity.

17

What to See

The City of New York is composed of five boroughs, four of which are on islands. Brooklyn and Queens (which houses JFK Airport) form the southern tip of Long Island, which stretches 118 miles (190km) north east to the summer social beach resorts around Easthampton. Small-town Staten Island sits in the harbour narrows between Brooklyn and New Jersey, an anchor of the Verrazano Bridge. The Bronx, north of Harlem, is the only borough on the mainland, the home of Yankee Stadium and the city's great zoo. Six million New Yorkers live in these

Really scraping the sky, the Empire State was once the tallest building in the world. Today, the spire is tops with tourists.

four boroughs. What visitors mean by 'New York' is, of course, the fifth borough, the turreted island metropolis 13½ miles (22km) long and 2 miles (3km) wide – Manhattan.

Midtown

ROCKEFELLER CENTER

The original 14 buildings of this famous midtown complex – known in pre-TV days as 'Radio City' – cover 12 acres (5ha) between Fifth Avenue and Avenue of the Americas (Sixth Avenue) from West 48th to 51st Streets. Today, however, **Rockefeller Center** encompasses some 22 acres (9ha) which include the skyscrapers on the west side of Avenue of the Americas from West 47th Street, all linked by vast underground concourses with shops, cafés, restaurants, a post office and the New York City subway.

Columbia University purchased the site in 1811 when it was farmland. In 1928, John D Rockefeller, a founder of the

Standard Oil Company, asked the university for a lease on the site to raise a commercial complex. Built between 1931 and 1940, Rockefeller Center houses multinational companies and attracts thousands of visitors and shoppers daily. It's so essential to New York – and America – that its purchase by the Japanese Mitsubishi group caused an uproar.

From Fifth Avenue you enter by the Channel Gardens, a sloping walkway divided by fountains and flower beds. Appropriately, the 'channel' lies **19** in between the Maison Française and the British Empire Building. At its end, the sunken Lower Plaza is a parasoled garden restaurant in summer, an ice-skating rink in winter. Watched over by a gold-leaf covered statue of Prometheus, the plaza is dominated by the Center's largest tower, the General Electric Building, still best known by its original name – the **RCA Building**. (Most New York skyscrapers are known by the corporation that built them or occupies the most office space. Wheeling and dealing over the recent decades has led to confusion as building names are continually changed.) A free walking-tour brochure, available at the information desk in the lobby at 30 Rockefeller Plaza, will guide you through the Center. On the underground concourse level, a video covers the Center's history, art and design.

The **Rainbow Room**, a truly magical Art Deco supper club and bar straight out of a 1930s movie, has fabulous views of the city from the 65th floor of the RCA Building (see p.76). Several floors are occupied by NBC, the radio and television network; a guided tour behind the scenes of the broadcasting studios starts at 30 Rockefeller Plaza (see p.132).

Radio City Music Hall, at Avenue of the Americas and West 50th Street, is the largest indoor movie theatre in the world, with a seating capacity

*E*very star's ambition is to play the nation's premier stage.

of around 6,000. A symbol of the period when everything Americans did had to be better – and above all bigger – Radio City holds all the records: the biggest chandeliers, the largest electric organ in the world ('the mighty Wurlitzer'), a revolving stage on three levels, plus lounges downstairs decorated in the most extravagant 1930s Art Deco style, and six miles of neon lighting.

Radio City mounts elaborate stage shows with seasonal themes. Featured performers are the Rockettes, America's most noted troupe of precision dancers. Backstage Hour-long tours of the Hall revolve around show schedules; for the latest current hours, call the tour desk on 632-4041, 10am-5pm seven days a week.

For a well-earned break on a hot summer's day, walk one block down West 50th Street to take in the refreshing sight of the Exxon Park waterfall and listen to a lunch-time musical performance. Small parks with fountains, plants and benches soften the cityscape in many midtown blocks.

FIFTH AVENUE

Fifth Avenue suggests luxury not just in the US, but all over the world. In the late 19th century, newly rich families built their mansions and brownstone houses between 34th and 50th Streets. After World War I, the section facing Central Park became fashionable, and quality shops and department stores moved into midtown. With the exception of Lord & Taylor, still in place at 38th Street, those best known for women's wear are to be found between 50th and 58th Streets – Saks Fifth Avenue (at 50th Street), Henri Bendel (between 55th and 56th Streets), Bergdorf Goodman (north of 57th Street) and a branch of the Galeries Lafayette in the Trump Tower (56th Street).

Donald Trump, a real estate entrepreneur whose personal peccadillos are rarely absent from the tabloid press, is responsible for the gaudy, lofty atrium of his **Trump Tower**, where a 'wall' of water slides down rose marble set between gleaming brass escalator rails. **21**

NEW YORK HIGHLIGHTS

(See also Museum Highlights on p.81)

United Nations

First Ave at 46th St; tel. 963-7713. New York's claim to be capital of the world is validated by the awesome presence of the UN headquarters in the heart of Manhattan. John D Rockefeller Jr donated the land, and architects Wallace K Harrison, Le Corbusier and Oscar Niemeyer designed the complex. (See p.32)

Empire State Building

350 Fifth Ave; tel. 736-3100. The most famous skyscraper in New York, offering unrivalled views from its observatories, and a movie star in its own right (*King Kong, Sleepless in Seattle...*), the Empire State is one of the most visited buildings in New York. Open 9.30am-11.30pm daily, restricted opening hours Christmas and New Year's Eve. Elevators to 86th floor observation deck $3.75. (See p.33)

World Trade Center

Chambers St, Rector St; tel. 435-3540. The twin towers dominate the skyline, and vertiginous views are on offer at WTC2. A 'must' in the Wall Street area. Open daily 9.30am-9.30pm in winter, 9.30am-11.30pm in summer. Elevators to observation deck £3.95. (See p.38)

South Street Seaport

Fulton St; tel. 669-9424. This regenerated district is a hit with families: below-the-deck tours of ancient ships, Children's Center museum of marine creatures, shops galore and excellent sea food. Museums and most shops open 10am-5pm daily except public holidays, restaurants and pubs open until late at night. (See p.43)

Central Park

Miles of driveways, bridle paths, bicycle lanes, walks and several other attractions are set in acres of 'natural' landscape for the delight of locals and visitors alike. The Visitors Center in the Dairy (*right*) is open Mar-Nov 11am-5pm Tue-Sun (1pm-5pm Fri) and Nov-Mar 11am-4pm Tue-Sun (1pm-4pm Fri). (See p.55)

Greenwich Village

Go through Washington Arch (*right*) and enter New York's most atmospheric neighbourhood. Great for eating, shopping, or just soaking up the atmosphere. (See p.48)

Ellis Island/Statue of Liberty

Circle Line or Statue of Liberty Ferry from Battery Park; tel. 363-3200. A worldwide symbol of liberty, New York's First Lady attracts thousands of admirers. Open daily 9am-5pm except 25 December. Ferry ticket: $6 adults, $5 seniors, $3 children. (See p.90)

At the bottom of the five-storey atrium is a sunken café. From this very space an only-in-New York transition leads to the adjoining IBM Building through a bamboo forest under glass. The jewellers Cartier, Tiffany & Co, Bulgari and Van Cleef & Arpels are nearby, as are boutiques of the top couturiers and famous leather goods stores, as well as a number of excellent bookshops.

West 47th Street between Fifth and Sixth Avenues is a famous international centre of the retail diamond trade. The area is dominated by Orthodox Jews, many dressed in long black coats and black hats.

St Patrick's Cathedral, set between East 50th and 51st Streets, was majestic when it was built, between 1858 and 1874. Today, however, it appears somewhat dwarfed by the skyscrapers of Rockefeller Center and the Olympic Tower apartments next door. Seat of the Archdiocese of New York, the church is the focal point of the Irish parade on St Patrick's Day, 17 March. In recent years it has also been a confrontation

flash point during the June Lesbian and Gay Pride parade.

The vast Grand Army Plaza, at the corner of Central Park South (at W 59th St), marks the division between the shopping area of Fifth Avenue and the residential section, lined with mansions and exclusive apartment buildings. You will pass by on your way to one of the uptown museums, and this is the place to hire a horse-drawn carriage for a ride round Central Park (see pp.55 and 129). It's also the site of two of New York's smartest hotels, the Plaza and the Pierre (at East 61st Street). Across from the Plaza, set a little way back from the avenue, is the General Motors Building and the giant toy store, FAO Schwartz.

Just one block east of Fifth Avenue, **Madison Avenue** has become synonymous with the world of advertising. It is perhaps equally famous for high fashion boutiques, art galleries and antique shops. Madison does have its share of skyscrapers, notably Philip Johnson's controversial AT&T postmodernist offices (today the Sony

Building), also nicknamed the 'Chippendale Building' for its curlicue crest. The 57-storey tower of the New York Palace hotel (between East 50th and 51st Streets) incorporates rather incongruously the neo-Renaissance Villard Houses, a New York landmark since 1885.

In a changing cityscape, St Patrick's Cathedral is timeless (right). Fifth Avenue parades spotlight the city's ethnic diversity (below).

IL CLUB ITALIANO
OF
WESTCHESTER COMMUNITY
COLLEGE

TIMES SQUARE AND BROADWAY

Pulsing **Times Square**, crossed by Broadway, stretches from the north side of West 42nd Street to West 47th Street. This is the heart of the Theater District, with first-run playhouses, movie theatres, nightclubs, restaurants, hotels and shops. The area has had a face-lift and is regaining much of the fabled Broadway dazzle, but it still has some of the city's nastiest strip clubs and sex shops.

The square throbs with the flashing multi-coloured lights of enormous advertising panels. Between 42nd and 43rd Streets, a moving illuminated tape made up of over 12,000

World-famous Broadway, long synonymous with New York's Theater District, pulses through Times Square.

light bulbs carries news head-lines continuously around the triangular building that used to house the *New York Times*. On 31 December, a lighted globe comes down a pole on its roof, announcing the arrival of the New Year, to be greeted by the tens of thousands of New Yorkers and visitors thronging the square below.

In Times Square, not all ac-tivity is above ground. Under-neath, where several subway lines and a crosstown shuttle towards Grand Central Termi-nal converge, aspiring musi-cians play for tips from the ceaselessly circulating crowds.

The metaphor for the New York theatre is **Broadway**. The city's biggest shows (at the very highest prices) are put on in a handful of auditoriums on Broadway itself, like the Win-ter Garden (1634 Broadway), but most 'on-Broadway' plays are performed at the theatres on its side streets between West 44th and 53rd Streets and at Lincoln Center in Upper West Side; 7.5 million tickets are sold each season. Off-Broad-way theatres, with auditoriums

of one hundred to 499 seats, and Off-Off-Broadway thea-tres, with fewer than a hundred seats, charge lower prices; these descriptions have nothing to do with geographical location, but differentiate between the mainstream and the more off-beat, less commercial produc-tions. (See also p.101.)

Ever since the 1890s, Car-negie Hall (Seventh Avenue at West 57th Street), has been the nation's premier concert stage, even though the New York Philharmonic Orchestra is now based at Lincoln Center (see p.54). Backstage tours are of-fered on Monday, Tuesday, Thursday and Friday.

42ND STREET

Traditionally, **42nd Street** is the most important crosstown street, and 42nd and Fifth Av-enue is the city's centre. In re-ality, the famous thoroughfare began to lose prestige in the 1960s, when the ocean liners no longer docked at its Hudson River end, and when its west-side was taken over by sleazy horror-and-porno cinemas; on **27** the east side the better hotels and businesses followed Manhattan's persisting power-centre shift northward.

A low point was eventually reached when plans were announced to erect an office building on top of Grand Central Terminal (see opposite), one of the city's genuine architectural masterpieces. Alarmed citizenry, including Jacqueline Kennedy Onassis, galloped to the rescue of the railway station, and Grand Central is now a

protected monument – this event turned the tide of decline.

A 42nd Street Improvement Association has made real progress cleaning up 'Sin Street', the stretch west of Broadway. Ten porn theatres have been closed and their entrance canopies bear whimsical and inspirational mottoes ('Turn soft and lovely anytime you have a chance', 'What urge will save us, now that sex won't?' 'It is embarrassing to be caught and killed for stupid reasons') all sponsored by the association.

Going east, the upgrading continues at West 42nd Street and Sixth Avenue, with the swooping ski-jump silhouette of the 1974 WR Grace Building. The architect who built it, Gordon Bunshaft, designed an almost identical building on 57th Street, a few steps from Fifth Avenue. Across the way is the green and leafy, newly restored oasis of Bryant Park, a great sunning spot for local office workers. Concerts are often staged there at noon; several kiosks sell tasty gourmet snacks as well as cut-rate concert and dance tickets.

*G*rand Central's vault (right) handles thousands of commuters
28 hurrying for their trains (above).

The park lies behind the **New York Public Library**, an American Beaux-Arts (neo-classical) style building inaugurated in 1911; two famous and much-photographed stone lions guard the Fifth Avenue entrance. One of the largest libraries in the world, it houses several million books, almost as many manuscripts, and vast reading rooms; it's a favourite with browsers and serious researchers alike. Changing exhibitions are regularly mounted in Gottesman Hall, the Berg Exhibition Room, and various other local galleries.

A little further east, an elevated ramp carries Park Avenue traffic around the massive bulk of **Grand Central Terminal**, completed in 1913 and a great Beaux-Arts masterpiece. Inside, 66 rail lines arrive on the upper level, 57 on the lower. The central concourse, vast, but also light, airy and harmonious under a star-painted ceiling 12 storeys high, is invaded every afternoon from 4 to 6pm by hundreds of thousands of suburban commuters catching their trains home. Not everyone standing in line is waiting to buy a train ticket, though; **29** one window sells chances on the popular New York State Lottery, whose top prize gets up into the millions of dollars.

A network of passageways links Grand Central to nearby hotels, office buildings and the subway. They're lined with all kinds of shops and several restaurants, including, at the lower level, the Oyster Bar & Restaurant, a New York institution, famous for its clam chowder (see p.75). The station is also one place in midtown where you are sure to find a restroom.

Farther east on 42nd Street stands the most beautiful sky-scraper of all, the **Chrysler Building**, a silvery Art Deco needle completed in 1930. For a few months it was the tallest structure in the world, with a height of 1,046ft (319m), but it was rapidly surpassed by the Empire State Building. The stylized eagle heads on the upper corners were modelled on the Chrysler automobile's 1929 radiator cap.

At the corner of Second Avenue, more Art Deco architecture distinguishes the Daily News Building. Television has crushed the once-lively daily mass circulation newspapers of

The Chrysler Contest

William Van Alen designed the Chrysler Building as a fitting monument to Walter Percy Chrysler's achievements in the automobile industry. It was to be the highest office building in the world. However, during its construction it was challenged by the Bank of the Manhattan Co Building, whose architect added a flagpole, thus overtaking the Chrysler Building by 2ft (60cm). Van Alen countered this move by adding a spire, making the Chrysler Building 1,046ft (320m) tall when completed in 1930. After this bitter fight the Chrysler Building was only in the book of records for a few months – in 1931 it was surpassed by the Empire State Building (see p.33).

*T*he Beaux Arts Terminal and Art Deco Chrysler tower are listed amongst the gems of New York's architecture.

New York, reduced to three to-day: the august, revered *New York Times*, the tabloid *Daily News*, and the perennially bank-rupt *New York Post* (not to mention *Newsday*, printed on Long Island for suburbia, and the nationally circulated *Wall Street Journal* and *USA Today*). An enormous revolving globe occupies a good part of the *Daily News* lobby. Well worth a look are the Ford Foundation headquarters between First and Second Avenues: offices give onto a spacious interior court planted with trees – actually the first New York atrium.

THE UNITED NATIONS

The eastern end of 42nd Street used to be a warren of tene-ments and slaughterhouses till John D Rockefeller Jr bought and donated the 18-acre (7ha)

*N*ew York prides itself on being the capital of the world. Dele-gates from 159 nations debate in the UN's General Assembly.

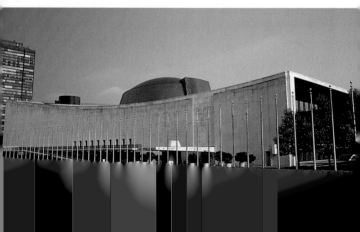

site after World War II in order to persuade the members of the **United Nations** to set up their headquarters – temporarily located in Queens near LaGuardia Airport at Flushing Meadows – in Manhattan. A team of 11 architects, including the American Wallace K Harrison, the Swiss Le Corbusier and the Brazilian Oscar Niemeyer, designed the buildings, which were completed in the early 1950s. The Secretariat is housed in the glass and marble upright domino, while the General Assembly meets in the round lower building with the slightly concave roof. In 1994, 159 flags of member nations fluttered from the flagpoles along First Avenue.

The 1993 bombing of the International Trade Center in downtown Manhattan and the subsequent discovery of an alleged plot to blow up various New York installations, including the UN headquarters, have sadly caused the authorities to suspend tours of the UN indefinitely. However, all is not lost: visitors can still study the sculptures in the 18-acre (7ha) grounds overlooking the East River and Queens, take in documentary exhibits on the walls by the visitors' entrance and buy books and souvenirs in the shops – there's a shop specializing in crafts from all over the world, where you'll be able to find original gifts at reasonable prices, and an adjoining bookshop selling UN publications. Another pleasure which remains is pausing in the meditation room adorned with stained-glass windows by Marc Chagall.

THE EMPIRE STATE BUILDING

The Empire State is no longer the tallest building in the world, but who knows the name of the record holder? (The Sears Tower, out in Chicago, is 40ft/12m higher.) Standing alone at nondescript low-rise Fifth Avenue and West 34th Street, the **Empire State Building** is everything a skyscraper should be, with 102 storeys; 60,000 tons of steel; 3,500 miles (5,632km) of telephone wires and cables; 60 miles (97km) of pipes; and **33**

a total volume of 1¼ million cubic yards (1 million cubic metres); 1,860 steps – not forgetting its towering height, at 1,414ft (431m), including the TV antenna (half as tall again as the Eiffel Tower). Opened in 1931 in the depths of the Great Depression, it took two years to complete. The viewing floors are the best place for an idea of New York's layout.

To reach the observation deck you first have to go down to the basement level, where you buy your ticket and get in line. While you're at the ticket office, why not take a look at the amazing **Guinness World of Records** exhibition? The museum features life-size displays of world-record holders, videos, and a data bank on sports, space, science and music superlatives.

An elevator will speed you up to the 80th floor in less than a minute. You'll just have time to catch your breath and get your ears unblocked before taking a second elevator to the 86th floor – 1,050ft (320m) above street level. In winter you can stay inside the heated shelter of the observatory; in summer enjoy the view from the outside terrace. On a clear day, it's possible to make out the funnels of ships 40 miles (65km) out to sea.

The Empire State's mast was the scene of King Kong's final battle – and ultimate death.

A third, last elevator completes the trip up the tower to the 102nd floor, right up where King Kong swatted at wasp-like attacking airplanes. The tower was built as a mooring for dirigibles that never came.

Back on earth, the area near the Empire State Building has some of New York's most popular stores. Go west along 34th Street into the wholesale Garment District for Macy's and the A&S Plaza (see p.96).

Nearby, at Seventh Avenue and West 33rd Street, is **Madison Square Garden**, renowned for boxing matches and various entertainment attractions, including the circus. In addition to being home to the New York Knickerbockers ('Knicks' – basketball) and the Rangers (ice hockey), it is also used as a conference centre. The Garden seats 20,000 people and the Felt Forum can take an additional 5,000.

Under Madison Square Garden is **Pennsylvania Station** (referred to as Penn Station), the railway terminal for New Jersey and Long Island commuters and for Amtrak trains

to the rest of the country. The former Penn Central Railway yard is now the site of the city's newest convention centre: an impressive black glass structure designed by architect IM Pei and named after a feisty New Yorker and long-time senator, Jacob Javits.

The East Side

Directly behind Grand Central and linked to it by escalators is the **MetLife Building**, originally built for the now-defunct Pan American Airlines. New Yorkers lament that the symmetry of Park Avenue – which approaches the north side of Grand Central through arches under the elegant, gold-topped Helmsley Building, once the New York Central Railroad headquarters – was spoiled by the 59-floor octagonal MetLife slab which now looms over it.

Park Avenue landmarks include the Waldorf-Astoria Hotel (located between East 49th and 50th Streets), host to distinguished personalities since 1931, and also the bronze-and- **35**

*A*bsolutely everything, from buttons to boats, is sold under one roof at 'Bloomie's', the Queen of East Side stores.

glass Seagram Building (between East 52nd and 53rd Sts), a 1958 pacesetter by Mies Van der Rohe and Philip Johnson.

Around the corner, the striking **Citicorp Center** (East 53rd Street between Lexington and Third Avenues) brings a rich and surprising touch to the skyline with its dramatically sloping silver roof. At ground level

is a lively three-storey 'market' of shops and restaurants set around a skylit central courtyard. The Citicorp skyscraper was built on the site of St Peter's Church, the 'jazz church' where Louis Armstrong's memorial service was held. Part of the deal was to replace old St Peter's with the present polygonal chapel decorated by the sculptor Louise Nevelson. A schedule of the fine free jazz concerts regularly held at the church is posted by the door.

The architecture along this stretch of Lexington Avenue could be Fritz Lang's futuristic silent film *Metropolis* brought to life. The variety of styles unleashed during the building boom of the 1970s is unique – enamelled ovals in brown and mauve, cones and cupolas, and even one nicknamed 'the lipstick building' for its shape and colours. Third Avenue still has a few of the low brick buildings that used to house Irish pubs; the classic, PJ Clarke's at 55th Street (see p.76), is protected by Landmark status and attracts a constantly renewed youthful clientele.

The East Side is an important shopping area, great for browsing. Top men's stores are found along Madison Avenue, beginning with the long-established Brooks Brothers at 43rd Street and followed by Paul Stuart, Tripler's and Barney's. The Queen of East Side stores, **Bloomingdale**'s, takes up the block between 59th and 60th Streets on Lexington Avenue. Behind 'Bloomie's', on Third Avenue, is a string of first-run movie theatres. The East 60s and 70s brownstone houses are home to New York's upper crust, and many of the city's 'in' (expensive) bistros and restaurants are located nearby.

Today, only a few restaurants remain to identify Yorkville, the area around East 86th Street, as the former German, Czech and Hungarian sector of Manhattan. The residence of the Mayor, **Gracie Mansion**, at East End Avenue and 88th Street, sits in Carl Schurz Park overlooking the East River. Parts of the Carl Schurz Park are built over the Franklin D Roosevelt Drive, which skirts the eastern shore of Manhattan from the Triborough Bridge exit, coming from Queens, to South Street.

For information and details of organized tours of the much-restored 18th-century manor in Federal style and its collection of furniture on loan from museums, call 570-4751 (tours take place on Wednesday only, reservations required). **37**

Downtown

WALL STREET AREA

Lower Manhattan, once nearly empty when the stockbrokers went home, has become one of New York City's most popular tourist destinations, thanks to the pull of the twin towers of the **World Trade Center**. These blunt monoliths spell P-O-W-E-R and do their best to dominate the rest of the skyline. Their symbolism earned them the terrorist bomb in an underground garage that sent

50,000 office workers into the street in 1993, trapped many in elevators and closed the Center's hotel and lofty Windows on the World restaurant for almost a year. Security is now very tight, but visitors are undeterred. The line for tickets and elevators to the viewing platform of Number Two still takes a good half hour.

Not (quite) the tallest buildings in the world (see p.33), the figures remain nevertheless impressive: 1,350ft (411m) high, with 43,600 windows. Each tower is designed to sway 3ft (2.7m) in the wind and contains 23 express and 72 local elevators. At the 107th floor of WTC2 there is an indoor viewing deck and snack bar.

Escalators then lead up three more storeys to the open roof and its breathtaking **view** – as good as from a helicopter. An electrified fence now prevents anyone crazy enough from trying to duplicate the feat of funambulist Philippe Petit, who walked a tightrope between the two buildings, in 1974; another 'human fly' daredevil managed to climb the tower using suction cups. Looking north and east to the East River towards midtown you'll see a

Take to the water... A boat ride puts Lower Manhattan's profile in perspective.

*N*YPD Blues? With so much going on in NYC, officers of the law have their work cut out.

vast brick-brown area stretching from 14th to 34th Streets, the Peter Cooper Village and Stuyvesant Town housing complex, and also the Bellevue Hospital compound.

At the base of the towers, numerous restaurants, concerts and art works divert lunchtime dawdlers and visitors. A TKTS stand in the WT2 mezzanine sells cut-rate same-day theatre tickets from 11am to 5.30pm, Monday through Friday – unlike the TKTS stand on Times Square, you rarely have to wait. A farmer's market set up in front of the plaza on Thursday (in the summer on Tuesday) provides a surprisingly human touch to the scene. Underneath the square are subway stations, banks and shops in a concourse that links seven buildings in the vast complex.

Another agreeable contrast across Church Street is the peaceful green glade of **St Paul's Chapel** and its churchyard. George Washington worshipped in the rose and white Federal-style chapel after his inauguration and until the US capital was moved to Philadelphia in 1790.

When the WTC was being built in 1970, some 30 million tons of excavated landfill was dumped on adjoining Hudson River docks to create the site of what would become, in the 1980s, **Battery Park City**, an attractive collection of high-

and low-rise apartment houses and parks. An esplanade along the river dotted with pretty waterfalls, plane trees, ponds and boat basins leads to a tall glassed-in Winter Garden with real palms ringed by quality shops, restaurants and bars. Free concerts are held here in winter. A pedestrian bridge connects the Winter Garden to the World Trade Center. In good weather the outdoor cafés around the yacht moorings here are a great spot for watching the sun go down over New Jersey as boats and ships sail by.

The grass, trees and monuments of breezy Battery Park cover the southernmost tip of Manhattan. Its centrepiece is **Castle Clinton**, once a battery of guns that, together with a similar fort a mere cannon-shot away on the Governor's Island Coast Guard base, controlled New York Harbor in the early 1800s. In fact, the guns were never fired in anger and the fort became a theatre where dignitaries such as Lafayette and Kossuth were fêted. From 1850 to 1892 it was the main point of entry through which seven

million immigrants filtered until Ellis Island took over. After housing the city's Aquarium (now in Coney Island) for several generations, Castle Clinton was recently restored to its original condition.

Tickets to the nearby **Statue of Liberty–Ellis Island ferry** are purchased here (see p.91). The **Staten Island Ferry** dock adjoins Battery Park. The 20-minute ride to Staten Island costs 50 cents for the round trip (you pay coming back); it gives photographers a classic shot of Manhattan's towers and the Statue of Liberty.

The skyscrapers in the narrow old streets of the Financial District are closer together than elsewhere and look all the more massive, turning the streets into veritable canyons. The heart of the district is **Wall Street**, which got its name from the wall of boards built here by the Dutch governor Peter Stuyvesant in 1653 to protect New Amsterdam from the Indians. It didn't do much good, however, because the settlers persisted in carting off planks for their own uses.

41

At the junction of Wall and Nassau Streets is the **Federal Hall National Memorial**. The original building, demolished in 1812, was the home of the United States Congress for a year. George Washington took the oath here as the first president of the United States, on 30 April 1789.

The **New York Stock Exchange**, across the way, was founded in 1792. The entrance at 20 Broad Street leads into a visitors' gallery, from where you will have a bird's-eye view of the controlled chaos of the trading floor and a commentary in several languages. You can learn about the workings of the Exchange from a permanent exhibition and a film.

It's strange to realize that **Trinity Church** at Broadway and Wall Street was long the tallest building in Manhattan – and that there is still room for God in a quarter so dedicated to Mammon. Trinity was built in 1846, but the parish itself goes back to 1697. Alexander Hamilton, one of the Founding Fathers and Washington's Secretary of the Treasury, is among the notables buried in the yard. Trinity Church is one of the city's richest landlords, with extensive holdings going back to colonial times. A large brass bull, the symbol of stockmarket optimists, is a popular snapshot backdrop at 26 Broadway. Further on, a triangular patch of what's left of Bowling Green is said to be the place where Peter Minuit bought Manhattan from the Indians for $24 in 1626 (see p.10).

The monumental **Old Customs House** here is now the home of the National Museum of the American Indian, the Hispanic Society of America and American Numismatic Society (see pp.88 and 132).

On the corner of Pearl and Broad streets stands the 18th-century **Fraunces Tavern**. On 4 December 1783, after the Revolutionary War was won, George Washington bade his officers farewell here, in the Long Room. Today, the Tavern is a museum, featuring early Americana and a programme of lectures and concerts.

Across Water Street, behind the old tavern, in the shadow

of towering skyscrapers, the Vietnam Veterans Plaza opens onto the East River. Right in its centre stands the evocative **Vietnam Veterans Memorial**, a 66ft (20m) long, 16ft (5m) high granite and glass block etched with quotations from letters and diaries written by US soldiers during that war.

Returning to Nassau Street, behind Federal Hall, admire the shining glass and aluminium tower of the Chase Manhattan Bank, built in 1961. Some 15,000 people work in this 65-storey edifice. The plaza displays sculpture by Isamu Noguchi and Jean Dubuffet.

A little further uptown, between Broadway and Park Row and looking both too elegant and too small for the turmoil it contains, is **City Hall**, built between 1803 and 1812. The offices of the Mayor of New York are here, and there's a collection of portraits and furniture from the federal period. Across Broadway and a little to the south stands the **Woolworth Building**, which reigned as the world's tallest building from 1913 until the Chrysler Building ushered in the skyscraper age in 1930.

SOUTH STREET SEAPORT

A prime example of New York's ability to renew itself is the **South Street Seaport Historic District**. This 11-acre (4ha), nine-block enclave on

*G*azing across Lower Manhattan, Miss Liberty holds high her lamp 'beside the Golden Door'.

43

the East River just below the Brooklyn Bridge was once in the middle of the nation's busiest working docks – today it may well be New York's liveliest tourist attraction.

From around 1800 to 1870 the waterfront here used to be a forest of masts; then steamships took to docking uptown on Hudson River piers. In the 1960s the South Street Seaport area was derelict and slated to be cleared for new skyscrapers. Instead, a team was brought in to restore the old trading houses on Fulton Street's 'Schermerhorn Row', refurbish the piers and period paving stones, close the area to traffic and create a maritime museum featuring a range of authentic ships from

the age of sail. The entrance is at Water and Fulton Streets.

This is a place to which the hackneyed phrase 'Fun for the whole family' really does apply. There's a Children's Center museum of marine creatures and crafts, an exhibit of model ships and half a dozen real ones to board. The prize is the four-masted barque *Peking*, with a

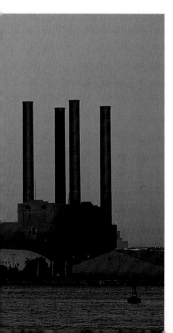

below-decks tour showing how sailors lived at sea as well as a film taken when the ship sailed through a gale around Cape Horn. You can actually sail the harbour on the schooner *Pioneer* (19th-century), a paddle-wheel steamer and a tug boat.

There are art galleries, craft demonstrations, walking tours, concerts on the piers, various shops, antique dealers and curio stalls. An infinite variety of food and drink is served at outdoor cafés and indoor restaurants, some specializing in seafood from the adjacent **Fulton Fish Market**. The wholesale market works at night; if you want to see it in action – and it is quite a sight – get there before 6am.

From Pier 17 you can get a good look at the **Brooklyn Bridge**, the first to span the river and the largest suspension bridge in the world when it was opened in 1883.

*T*he tidal East River separates the boroughs of Manhattan and Brooklyn, a world apart. **45**

Atmospheric Neighbourhoods

LOWER EAST SIDE

The remnants of the old Jewish quarter are located on the north-east side of Chinatown, beyond Hester Street, the site of the Jewish market at the end of the 19th century. Simply follow Hester Street eastwards and then walk north along Orchard Street and you'll see a shadow of the market's heyday. Dormant on the Sabbath from Friday evening to Saturday at sunset, the place springs to life on Sunday when it's invaded by Orthodox Jews in black hats and long frock coats pick their way among black and Hispanic vendors.

Memorabilia and historical photographs documenting the district's multi-ethnic past are exhibited in the **Lower East Side Tenement Museum** at 97 Orchard Street. Located in a 19th-century tenement, the museum conducts walking tours with commentary (for details, call 431-0233).

For a snack, select a pickle and a bulging pastrami (seasoned smoked beef) sandwich and a glass of seltzer (carbonated water) in one of the neighbourhood delis, or have a spring roll at Bernstein's kosher Chinese restaurant on Essex Street.

At the turn of the century, during the flood of immigration, newcomers moved in their thousands into the Lower East Side. Most of them stayed only a few years, long enough to learn English, find a job and set off to make a living elsewhere. Substantial groups of Jews, Chinese and Italians, however, chose to settle in their own enclaves. The Chinese are still here in strength, and the colours, sounds and smells of the other communities linger on.

CHINATOWN

If you take the Lexington Avenue Line subway to **Chinatown**, you cannot go wrong: the Canal Street Station has signs in both Roman and Chinese characters. The telephone booths have pagoda roofs, narrow shops sell ivory and jade jewellery, grocers display exotic Chinese produce, and innumerable restaurants feature regional specialities.

Well over 100,000 Chinese live in bustling Chinatown, a loosely defined area embracing Canal Street, Chatham Square and Mott Street. The earliest arrivals came to America in the 19th century, during the California Gold Rush and period of railway construction; most immigrants today come directly from Hong Kong. To learn about the history and sites of

the area, take the 90-minute-long walking tour conducted on Sunday from April to November by the Chinatown History Museum, at 70 Mulberry St. (The museum is open six days a week, Sunday-Friday and walking tours are offered on Sunday only; tel. 619-4785.)

Forming an intersection of ten streets in the southern part of Chinatown, the adjoining Chatham and Kimlau Squares are chaotic with both vehicular and pedestrian traffic. At the corner of Division Street and the Bowery (see p.52) stands a 1983 bronze statue of Confucius, and south of the squares, a few steps down St James's Place, are New York's oldest 'monuments', barely a dozen effaced but nonetheless touching tombstones, the remnants of the Shearith Israel Cemetery, founded here in 1656 by New York's first immigrants, Spanish and Portuguese Jews.

Chinatown, the largest Chinese community outside Asia, is still growing.

47

LITTLE ITALY

Little Italy has been getting littler over the years, as families of Italian descent have moved uptown or to the suburbs. The district traditionally centred on Mulberry Street now shares its southern part with an ever expanding Chinatown. The Italian section is now principally a gastronomic hub, with a range of expensive espresso bars and restaurants, moderately priced establishments, excellent bakeries and grocers specializing in home-made and imported Italian delicacies. The district is at its liveliest during the ten-day Feasts of Sant'Antonio in early June and San Gennaro, in September (see pp.106-7).

☑ GREENWICH VILLAGE

'The Village', as New Yorkers call **Greenwich Village**, has been separate, casual and very different from the rest of the city ever since its beginnings. It really was a distinct village called Greenwich in colonial times, then became a neighbourhood of conservative Geor-

gian brick houses with white trim over the doors and carriage barns in back-alley mews. A few of these houses remain, but conservative the Village isn't. A reputation for bohemian life-styles followed the arrival after World War I of artists and writers who found here cheap lodgings, inexpensive restaurants and speakeasies.

Today the lack of orthodoxy is maintained by the students of New York University on Washington Square, the gay community and the denizens of the many bookstores and old-time Village bars. Artists are harder to find, though every year at the Washington Square Outdoor Art Exhibit, a summertime tradition since 1931, hundreds of painters, sculptors and photographers display their works.

The limits of Greenwich Village run north–south from 14th Street to Houston Street and east–west from Broadway to the Hudson River. West of Avenue of the Americas it becomes the fairly genteel **West Village**; the youthful, raunchy, sometimes druggy and more overtly ethnic neighbourhood

48

GREENWICH VILLAGE

of East Village centres on St Mark's Place and roughly extends from Lafayette St to Avenue D and the East River.

The Village feeling begins at the Washington Arch and **Washington Square** at the foot of Fifth Avenue. Designed by architect Stanford White, the triumphal arch was erected in 1889 to mark the centenary of George Washington's inauguration as president. Washington Square Park is surrounded by the buildings of New York University and student residences; the elegant old houses on the north side of the square are the homes of professors.

Hidden away behind these august dwellings are two private lanes that used to lead to the stables belonging to Washington Square's wealthy residents: **Washington Mews**, one block up Fifth Avenue on your right, and **MacDougal Alley**, just a few steps up MacDougal Street from the north-western end of the square.

Walk west along 8th Street across Avenue of the Americas into a charming residential area **50** of small, tree-lined streets of

'brownstones' – so called because of their matching brick or brownish-red sandstone. All houses have a flight of stairs leading up to the door. Some of the Village's best antique dealers are clustered here, as well as quite a few cozy restaurants.

Follow Bleecker Street to the south-east and you will soon find the shopping strip of the neighbourhood, teeming with quaint craft and curio shops, bizarre second-hand clothing stores, cafés and small restaurants. For decades now, Christopher Street, west of Hudson Street, has been a focal point for the city's lesbian and gay community. The oldest gay bar in the city, the Stonewall, located at No. 53 Christopher Street, is considered a gay historical landmark. Indeed, it was from here, in the Stonewall Riot of 1968, that gays first began to fight back against police harrassment.

'*Colourful*' is the most appropriate word for Greenwich Village's people and places.

You should make at least two trips to the Village – by day to see the sights, and at night to catch the atmosphere, have dinner and listen to some jazz at the Village Vanguard or the Blue Note.

A separate community, **East Village** extends from Broadway eastward to First Avenue and beyond. Much less affluent than its big brother to the west, this neighbourhood nevertheless has its fair share of galleries, New Age bookshops and clothes stalls, night spots and small ethnic restaurants. As a matter of fact, purists claim that this is where the bohemian spirit of the Village is most authentic. Through the curtainless windows of its back streets, you might glimpse paintings or sculpture in the making.

At Lafayette Street, just to the south of Cooper Square, stands the building which once housed the first public library of New York. Nowadays it's the seat of the **Public Theater** (see p.101), a multi-auditorium complex and home of the New York Shakespeare Festival. The traditional and avant-garde film and theatre shows presented are always of high quality, and some now-famous plays tentatively launched here went on to become the longest running shows on Broadway.

A few blocks south from Lafayette Street, Great Jones St eastwards leads on to the **Bowery**, laid out by Peter Stuyvesant in the 17th century as the road to his farm (*bouwerij* in Dutch). In the 19th century this was New York's 'grand boulevard', lined with dance halls and beer taverns. These days, it's mostly given over to sordid hotels and the occasional wino. However, there are some good rock and jazz spots, and theatres have moved in. You need not be afraid to go there in the evening: the Bowery is much less dangerous than it looks.

To finish off, a final downtown church: on the very spot where the Stuyvesant family chapel once stood (East 10th St at Second Avenue), **St Mark's-in-the-Bowery**, built in 1799, is a charming church with some noteworthy stained-glass windows – and an extremely lively congregation.

SOHO AND TRIBECA

SoHo (short for South of Houston Street) is the area bound by Houston Street, Broadway, Canal Street and the river. It has become the Village's chic southern neighbour, with expensive cafés, restaurants and art galleries, and shops selling the very latest in fashion.

Its history has followed the pattern of the Village. Artists who couldn't afford the rents after the Village's commercialization moved south to the derelict lofts and warehouse floors of the industrial district of SoHo. The most successful were able to install kitchens, bathrooms and comfortable interiors, while others made do with bare walls and floors for the sake of ample space and light.

However, the success of the galleries on West Broadway – especially No. 420, where the old pillars of the pop art movement, Andy Warhol, Robert Rauschenberg and Roy Lichtenstein displayed their works – caused rents to soar. Interior decorators and gallery owners wasted no time in turning the

*E*choing London's Soho, New York's SoHo actually stands for South of Houston Street.

lofts and ground-floor apartments into expensive residential and commercial properties. The dealers moved in, and the artists moved out, many heading south-west to the derelict warehouses of the **TriBeCa** (Triangle Below Canal Street) neighbourhood. So close to the **53**

Financial District of the World Trade Center (see p.38) and Battery Park City (see p.40) with all its glitter and wealth, TriBeCa, too, has become a much sought after area, and art galleries, fashionable restaurants and trendy boutiques have duly blossomed.

Upper West Side

Manhattan's Upper West Side is the area west of Central Park and north of Columbus Circle (59th Street). It's a lively and mixed-up district, and it's also the part of New York that can claim most success in terms of racial integration. In this area, a hodgepodge of intellectuals and artists live side by side with blue-collar workers and shopkeepers of different ethnic backgrounds. In and around Columbus Avenue, between the renowned Lincoln Center and West 79th Street, prestigious stores, elegant boutiques, restaurants, popular art galleries and antique shops have taken over from the old neighbourhood establishments.

LINCOLN CENTER

It was the construction of the **Lincoln Center for the Performing Arts**, 62nd and 66th Streets west of Broadway, that launched the revival of the entire neighbourhood. In 1955 John D Rockefeller III put forward the proposal for a great cultural centre. It was to house both the Metropolitan Opera, the New York Philharmonic, the New York City Ballet and the Juilliard School of Music. The city bought the land and razed the Puerto Rican ghetto on the site. (The musical *West Side Story* was filmed here just before the change.)

Financed entirely by private funds, the Center covers an area of 12 acres (5ha). The plaza, a vast esplanade surrounding a fountain, acts as the focal point of the three major buildings. To the left is the New York State Theater, home of the New York City Ballet and the New York City Opera. Designed by architect Philip Johnson and built in 1964, it has a simple, stately façade complemented by a red and gold auditorium studded with crystal. The Metropolitan Opera House (the 'Met'), host to the Metropolitan Opera and the American Ballet Theater, was designed by Wallace K Harrison, completed in 1966 and can hold 3,800 people. It is the most beautiful building in the complex, with an airy front of glass highlighted by marble pillars. Two Chagall murals adorning the central lobby can be seen from the outside.

During the summer, open-air concerts are performed in the Guggenheim Bandshell in adjacent Damrosch Park. Facing the New York State Theater is Avery Fisher Hall, completed in 1962, also known as Philharmonic Hall. The New York Philharmonic and eminent visiting orchestras and soloists play here in an auditorium that seats approximately 2,700.

Just behind the hall, to the right of the Met, you can make out the outline of the Vivian Beaumont Theater, designed by Finnish-born architect Eero Saarinen. In addition to the delightful circular theatre, is the second, much smaller, Mitzi Newhouse Theater, originally intended to provide a base for a permanent American repertory company, along the lines of the Comédie Française in Paris. The plan never materialized, however.

Behind the Vivian Beaumont Theater, the New York Public Library for the Performing Arts at Lincoln Center includes a film archive and a file on actors, stars and directors.

Further back, but connected to Lincoln Center by a footbridge over West 65th Street, you'll come across the Juilliard School, one of the world's outstanding music conservatories, and the Walter Reade movie theatre. Alice Tully Hall on the ground floor is a concert hall where the best pupils often perform in afternoon concerts. It is also the home of the Chamber Music Society.

CENTRAL PARK

A vast green breathing space in the centre of Manhattan, half a mile wide and 2½ miles long (800m x 4km), **Central Park** acts both as a sports field, playground and picnic spot to tens **55** of thousands of city-dwellers daily. In the 1840s the poet William Cullen Bryant realized that New York needed more parks for its expanding population and launched a campaign to persuade the city to buy the land – then wasteland beyond the city limits, inhabited by squatters. Landscape architects Frederick Law Olmstead and Calvert Vaux won a competition to design the park. The project took 3,000 workers 16 years to complete.

Conceived in the English style, the park is entirely artificial but it doesn't look it: the Lake, the paths, the 'forests' and meadows the architects created might have been there since time immemorial. Four million trees were planted, now home to countless half-tame squirrels and numbers of opossums and racoons. By day it's perfectly safe to go walking in the park, but you should avoid it at night, unless you're going with the crowds to the outdoor summer theatre.

Starting from the south-east corner of the park, note how **56** the **Pond** reflects skyscrapers.

Check out the park's compact zoo, where a glass wall lets you see polar bears swimming. The sea lions perform for their fish at feeding time, 2pm and 4pm. If you have children in tow, show them the animated musical clock just outside.

Then call in at the **Dairy**, the Central Park Visitors' Center, for a calendar of events, which could include anything from free opera to a kite-flying contest. Drop in on the deeply absorbed chess players at the Chess House next door (pieces are available at the Dairy) and don't miss the terrific Carousel just a little farther west. From there, you'll be able to see softball games underway.

Across the West Drive at 66th Street, the Tavern on the Green's terrace is a good spot for a breather and some light refreshment. It used to house sheep that grazed on the broad Sheep Meadow here; now the

City stress just fades away on a Sunday afternoon in glorious Central Park.

Columbus Circle
Central Park West
West Drive
Strawberry Fields
Tavern on the Green
Heckscher Ball Fields
Lake
Sheep Meadow
Central Park West
Carousel
Chess and Checkers House
Central Drive
Volleyball Courts
Bow Bridge
Dairy
Central Park Visitor Center
Bethesda Fountain
Loeb Boathouse
Wollman Rink
Literary Walk and Mall
Pond
East Drive
Hans Christian Andersen Statue
Grand Army Plaza
Central Park Zoo
Alice in Wonderland Statue
Conservatory Water
Fifth Avenue
Frick Collection
(East 70th Street at Fifth Avenue)

meadow is perfect for picnics, frisbee tossing and sunbathing. Head east toward the trees and you'll come upon the Literary Walk (with a few undistinguished statues of writers) and the Mall leading to the Bethesda Fountain and Terrace, by the lakeside. In summer, you can lunch on the terrace of the Loeb Boathouse – to the right – and rent a bike, or a boat for a row on the Lake. At the oval Conservatory Water near Fifth Avenue, permit holders sail their miniature boats (as did the mouse, Stuart Little, in EB White's classic tale of the same name) next to statues of Hans Christian Andersen and Alice in Wonderland.

On a rise level with the Metropolitan Museum of Art (see p.64) stands Cleopatra's Needle, a 3,600-year-old obelisk (unconnected with Cleopatra) that was a gift from Egypt in the 19th century.

More recent is **Strawberry Fields** (at Central Park West between West 71st and 74th Sts), Yoko Ono's 'peace garden' memorial to her husband, John Lennon, shot in 1980 just

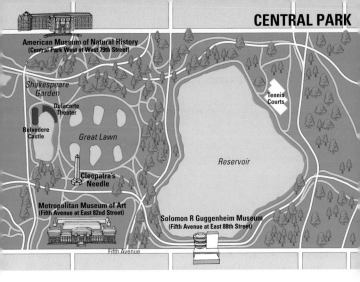

across the street, in front of the ponderous **Dakota** apartment house (1 West 72nd Street), home to many of New York's rich and famous.

The oval **Great Lawn** in the middle of the Park between the 79th and 86th Street transverses has held a million people lying on the grass to hear (free) opera, classical music and pop concerts. In its southwest corner, the open-air Delacorte Theater stages at 8pm in July and August Shakespeare-in-the-Park productions. To get the free tickets, stand in line for a numbered slip from 3pm of the performance date, then return at 6.15pm to stand in line again and exchange the number for a ticket. The leading roles are usually played by film and TV stars. Belvedere Castle, standing atop the rock behind the Delacorte, looks out over the park. It's a weather station and centre for conservation classes and nature outings for kids.

The 1½-mile (2.5km) path around the **Reservoir** is very popular with joggers. No longer needed for water supply, the **59** reservoir may eventually be filled in to add 106 more park acres (43ha).

For sport lovers, something is going on in the park every day, but most of all on Sunday in the summer. There are miles of riding, cycling and jogging paths, which can become ski trails in winter. There are 30 tennis courts (best approached from the West 96th Street entrance), two ice-skating rinks and adventure playgrounds for children. In the south-east sector of the park, at the **Wollman Memorial Rink**, you can rent skates and spin around the ice to music in winter; in summer rollerbladers take over and a miniature golf course opens.

COLUMBIA UNIVERSITY

the Protestant Episcopal Cathedral Church of St John the Divine, at Amsterdam Ave and West 112th St, is 'the world's largest Gothic-style cathedral'. Begun in 1892 and completed by 1939, it still employs stonecutters to hand-carve ornamentation. It is also known for its jazz and choral music series.

Beyond the cathedral lies the campus of **Columbia University**. Founded in 1754 as King's College, Columbia is a member of the Ivy League. Dwight D Eisenhower was its president for a while after World War II. The university is private and fee-paying, but its income from rented property enables it to offer a number of scholarships.

Straight across Broadway stands **Barnard College**, Columbia University's affiliated women's college, and behind it looms the stolid neo-Gothic Riverside Church. Its bell tow-

At the heart of the city, Central Park offers all kinds of sporting activities.

er, housing a 74-bell carillon, offers sweeping views over the cityscape. The temple-like edifice in Riverside Park at West 122nd Street is in fact Grant's Tomb, the mausoleum of General Ulysses S Grant, Commander-in-Chief of the Union Army in the Civil War and US President from 1869 to 1877.

Beside the park is **Riverside Drive**, lined with some great apartment houses looking out onto the Hudson River. They started life in the luxury class, dropped out of fashion, and are very much in demand again.

Harlem

Harlem, the spiritual capital of Black America, is a self-contained community with its rich, poor and middle-income sections, historical and cultural landmarks, attractive homes and many more sadly run-down slum streets. Outsiders, both black and white, steer clear of the latter districts.

Harlem has been steadily losing population over recent decades: in the 1950s it was the home of a million blacks; today barely a quarter of a million remain. Optimists attribute this exodus to housing programmes and the improvement in living standards; pessimists counterclaim that the poor have been forced out of Manhattan by the dilapidation of their ghetto, and have only gone as far as outlying districts – the Bronx and parts of Brooklyn. There's some truth in both arguments.

Harlem begins north of Central Park and extends to 178th Street, bounded on the west by Morningside and Washington Heights and on the north and east by the Harlem River connecting the Hudson and East Rivers. Its commercial centre is 125th Street and Lennox Avenue. For visitors, the best way to approach Harlem is by guided tour – contact the New York Convention & Visitors Bureau (see p.135) or the Harlem Visitors & Conventions Association, tel. 427-3317.

Harlem Spirituals Inc. (tel. 757-0425) offers a variety of weekday, Sunday and nighttime tours in English, French, **61**

German, Italian, Japanese or Spanish. Or loop through a section on the No. 1 bus, up Madison and down Fifth Avenue.

Founded by Dutch settlers, Harlem remained a village for a long time. As immigrants moved into the Lower East Side and the rich pre-empted midtown and beyond, many middle-class families moved north to Harlem. Some of their houses are now the homes of prosperous black families, notably in **St Nicholas Historic District** between Adam Clayton Powell Jr Boulevard and Frederick Douglass Boulevard on 138th and 139th Streets.

After World War I, New York was the Promised Land of jobs and civil rights for oppressed southern blacks, and Harlem rapidly became an all-black neighbourhood. In the Jazz Age of the 1920s and early 1930s, the Harlem nightclubs, such as the Cotton Club, were among the city's most popular. The Wednesday Amateur Night at the **Apollo Theater** at 253 West 125th Street has been the launching pad for many musical careers, includ-

ing Ella Fitzgerald's, and even now it gives hopefuls a chance.

A drive through Harlem is included in many sightseeing tours of Manhattan and there are specialized tours, some run by blacks, to the cultural high spots and to hear gospel-singing in churches. The **Studio Museum of Harlem** (West 125th Street at Malcolm X Blvd) is dedicated to the arts and artefacts of black America and the Caribbean; there are also concerts and films and a museum shop. At Malcolm X Boulevard and West 135th Street, the **Schomburg Center for Research in Black Culture**, a public library and art museum, possesses one of the world's most important collections covering black history and African-American culture.

At Convent Avenue, between West 141st and 142nd Streets, the Hamilton Grange National Memorial was in the early 19th century the home of American Founding Father Alexander Hamilton. The stately **Morris-Jumel Mansion** and gardens (1765) at Jumel Terrace and West 161st Street exhibits period furniture in a beautifully restored setting. For some delicious soul food, head for Sylvia's (328 Lenox Ave), where you can sample typical South Carolina fare.

Americans of Hispanic origin are scattered in many parts of New York City's five boroughs, but **'El Barrio'** – the Quarter – in East (or Spanish) Harlem was the first predominantly Puerto Rican district. The Museo del Barrio (Fifth Avenue at East 104th Street) is devoted to the art and culture of this lively population.

Museums

The museums alone – there are more than 100 of them – qualify New York as one of the world's great cultural capitals. In this section, we have highlighted some of New York's best museums, and you'll find their addresses, phone numbers and opening hours listed on p.81 and pp. 130-2. On the whole, Manhattan's museums are clustered around Central Park and Midtown.

MAJOR MUSEUMS

American Museum of Natural History

This is the largest natural history museum in the world, containing 30 million artifacts and specimens. The *Tyrannosaurus rex* and other dinosaurs are currently the star exhibit, especially the **Barosaurus** exhibit, but don't miss the life-like dioramas of animals in their habitats, the full-size blue whale, the prehistoric shark jaws that could swallow a taxi, or the dazzling section on minerals and precious stones, featuring the Star of India – the largest sapphire ever found. Exhibits include human evolution and a treasury of primitive art.

The **Naturemax Theater**, a hall with a four-storey-high and 66ft (20m) wide screen, shows films on the wonders of the earth. The museum's shops are great and there are several areas serving food and drink, one called 'The Diner Saurus'.

The **Hayden Planetarium**, next door, has engrossing programmes about the stars and **63** space exploration. The Laserium (same building) has sound and light shows featuring the laser beam on Friday and Saturday evenings.

The Brooklyn Museum

The pre-Columbian art alone would make this an important museum, but the sections devoted to Egyptian, Far Eastern and Persian art are also exceptional. The costume museum is lovely, and the remaining rooms feature a permanent exhibition of American furniture from the time of the first settlers. The museum overlooks Prospect Park, where you can spend a pleasant afternoon.

Ellis Island Immigration Museum

See The Statue of Liberty and Ellis Island on pp.90-2.

✓ The Metropolitan Museum of Art

The 'Met' is a treasure house for all humanity, assembling **64** the best of every civilization, a collection of collections, any one of which would make another museum great. It has nearly 250 rooms; 4,500 paintings and drawings; a million prints; 4,000 musical instruments; and countless pieces of furniture and sculpture. Only a quarter of the collection is on display at any one time.

You cannot expect to skim over the whole museum in one visit – concentrate on one or two collections at a time, and you'll come away enriched and not too exhausted. Make your choice from the maps at the foot of the great central staircase. You can rent portable cassette players providing commentary for various halls.

Where to begin? Medieval armour and weapons? Etruscan urns? Japanese screens or Persian carpets? Mesopotamian gold ornaments? High fashion dresses and fabrics of the roaring 20s? Rembrandts, Picassos, El Grecos, Cézannes? They are all here, in ranks with their peers. To make things a little easier, the Met usually has one or more special exhibitions, so try looking at these first.

Hotels and Restaurants in New York

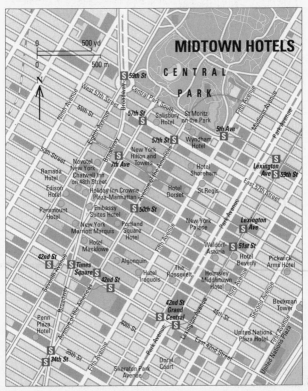

MIDTOWN HOTELS

CENTRAL PARK

500 yd
500 m

N

West 57th Street

Central Park South

59th St

57th St

Salisbury Hotel

St Moritz on the Park

5th Ave

55th St

Ninth Avenue

Eighth Avenue

Broadway

57th St

New York Hilton and Towers

Wyndham Hotel

7th Ave

Hotel Shoreham

Lexington Ave 59th St

50th Street

Novotel New York

Ramada Hotel

Chatwell Inn on 48th Street

Hotel Dorset

St Regis

Fifth Avenue

Madison Avenue

Park Avenue

Edison Hotel

Holiday Inn Crowne Plaza-Manhattan

East 57th Street

Paramount Hotel

Embassy Suites Hotel

50th St

New York Palace

Lexington Ave

New York Marriott Marquis

Portland Square Hotel

Park Avenue

Waldorf-Astoria

51st St

Hotel Macklowe

Algonquin

Fifth Avenue

Helmsley Middletown Hotel

Hotel Beverly

Pickwick Arms Hotel

42nd St

Times Square

Hotel Iroquois

The Roosevelt

Third Avenue

Beekman Tower

Seventh Avenue

Broadway

42nd St

45th St

Second Avenue

Penn Plaza Hotel

Avenue of the Americas

40th St

42nd St Grand Central

Lexington Avenue

United Nations Plaza Hotel

First Avenue

United Nations Plaza

35th St

34th St

Fifth Avenue

Park Avenue

East 42nd Street

Sheraton Park Avenue

Doral Court

65

Recommended Hotels

Hotel prices are, by most standards, high. However, almost all hotels offer weekend packages with reductions of 20 to 50 percent. These may include free museum passes, theatre tickets and brunch or dinner. Special rates, at a discount of about 20-25 percent, are available during slow times such as in summer. Reserve your room in advance. Many hotels offer fax and toll-free (1-800 numbers) services for making your reservations.

   Most rooms have double or twin beds, whether for single or double occupancy – the incremental charge for double occupancy is only 10-20 percent. The prices below are based on a midweek night, double occupancy of an average room, and do not include taxes (see p.116) and tips. All rooms have bathrooms en suite. Most hotels have individual climate controls, cable TV and direct-dial phones. Breakfast is rarely included.

III	above $250
II	$125-250
I	below $125

MIDTOWN

The Algonquin III
59 W 44th St, NY 10036
Tel. 840-6800/1-800-548-0345
Fax 944-1419
Truly a literary landmark. Renowned cabaret. 165 small rooms.

Beekman Tower III
3 Mitchell Place
off First Ave at 49th St, NY 10016
Tel. 355-7300/1-800-637-8483
Fax 779-7068
Comfortable hotel, popular with diplomats. Great views. 171 rooms.

Chatwal Inn on 48th St I
234 W 48th St, NY 10036
(Broadway and Eighth Ave)
Tel. 246-8800/1-800-826-4667
Fax 974-3922
Handsome Theater District hotel. Striking lobby with sky-lit atrium and a waterfall. 400 rooms.

Doral Court II
130 E 39th St, NY 10016
(at Lexington Ave)
Tel. 685-1100/1-800-22-DORAL
Fax 889-0287
Pretty hotel in a residential area. Spacious rooms. 199 rooms.

Edison Hotel ||

228 W 47th St, NY 10036
Tel. 840-5000/1-800-637-7070
Fax 719-9541
A serviceable, long-established and reasonably priced Theater District hostelry. 1,000 rooms.

Embassy Suites Hotel ||

1568 Broadway at 47th St
NY 10036
Tel. 719-1600/1-800-EMBASSY
Fax 921-5212
Suites with king-size beds, convertible couch; kitchenette; free newspaper, breakfast and cocktails (5.30-7.30pm). 460 rooms.

The Helmsley Middletowne Hotel ||

148 E 48th St, NY 10017
(Lexington and Third Aves)
Tel. 755-3000/1-800-221-4982
Fax 832-0261
Quiet and very comfortable lodgings near the UN. 192 rooms.

Holiday Inn Crowne Plaza-Manhattan ||

1605 Broadway at 48th St
NY 10019
Tel. 977-4000/1-800-243-6969
Fax 333-7393
Great views and biggest hotel pool in New York City. Non-smoking rooms and rooms designed for the disabled. 770 rooms.

Hotel Beverly ||

125 E 50th St, NY 10022
(at Lexington Ave)
Tel. 753-2700/1-800-223-0945
Fax 759-7300
A family-owned establishment in a convenient, busy East Side location. 187 rooms.

Hotel Dorset |||

30 W 54th St, NY 10019
Tel. 247-7300; fax 581-0153
Dignified establishment situated near Fifth Avenue shops, around the corner from the Museum of Modern Art. 210 rooms.

Hotel Iroquois |

49 W 44th St, NY 10036
(Fifth and Sixth Aves)
Tel. 840-3080/1-800-332-7220
Fax 398-1754
Pleasantly renovated and centrally located hotel. Convenient suites offer fully equipped kitchenettes. 100 rooms.

Hotel Macklowe |||

145 W 44th St, NY 10036
(Sixth Ave and Broadway)
Tel. 768-4400/1-800-622-5569
Fax 768-0847
52-storey contemporary Art Deco tower situated off Times Square. Guest rooms fitted with high-tech electronics, and excellent health club. 638 rooms.

67

The New York ‖-‖‖
Hilton and Towers
1335 Avenue of the Americas at
54th St, NY 10019-6078
Tel. 586-7000/1-800-445-8667
Fax 315-1374
The biggest: restaurants, nightclub
and fitness center under one roof.
Airport bus stop. 2,042 rooms.

The New York ‖-‖‖
Marriott Marquis
Broadway between 45th and
46th Sts, NY 10036-4017
Tel. 398-1900
Fax 704-8969
Tourist/business hotel close to the
theatres. New York's only revolving rooftop restaurant. Airport bus
stop. 1,871 rooms, 111 suites.

The New York Palace ‖‖
455 Madison Ave, NY 10022
(E 50th and 51st Sts)
Tel. 888-7000/1-800-221-4982
Fax 303-6000
Behind St Patrick's Cathedral. This
modern tower incorporates the re-
stored Villard Houses. 963 rooms.

Novotel New York ‖
226 W 52nd St on Broadway
NY 10019
Tel. 315-0100/1-800-221-3185
Fax 765-5363
NY branch of European chain in
the thick of Broadway. 474 rooms.

Paramount Hotel ‖
235 W 46th St, NY 10036
(Broadway and Eighth Ave)
Tel. 764-5500/1-800-225-7474
Fax 354-5237
A stylish, well equipped Theater
District hotel with a health club,
VCRs offered in all rooms, video
library and children's playroom.
610 rooms.

Penn Plaza Hotel ‖
215 W 34th St, NY 10001
Tel. 947-5050/1-800-633-1911
Fax 268-4892
Small and clean budget hotel lo-
cated in the bustling Garment Dis-
trict close to the Javits Convention
Center. 76 rooms.

Pickwick Arms Hotel ‖
230 E 51st St, NY 10022
(Second and Third Aves)
Tel. 355-0300/1-800-742-5945
Fax 755-5029
Attractive budget hotel in residen-
tial area. 385 rooms, some with
shared bathrooms.

Portland Square Hotel ‖
132 W 47th St, NY 10036
(Sixth and Seventh Aves)
Tel. 382-0600
Fax 382-0684
Nicely restored 1904 Theater Dis-
trict hotel. 110 rooms, some with
shared bathrooms.

Ramada Hotel ||

790 Eighth Avenue, NY 10024
(W 48th and 49th Sts)
Tel. 581-7000/1-800-572-6232
Fax 974-0291

This 15-storey hostelry has clean rooms and an open-air rooftop swimming pool. 366 rooms.

The Roosevelt ||

Madison Avenue at 45th St
NY 10017
Tel. 661-9600/1-800-223-1870
Fax 661-4475

A solid, spacious standby and midtown meeting place. A favourite with businessmen, near Grand Central. 995 rooms.

Salisbury Hotel ||

123 W 57th St, NY 10019
(Sixth and Seventh Aves)
Tel. 246-1300/1-800-223-0680
Fax 977-7752

Two blocks south of Central Park, the Salisbury offers pleasant and spacious rooms. 320 rooms.

The Sheraton ||||
Park Avenue

45 Park Avenue at 37th St
NY 10016
Tel. 685-7676/1-800-325-3535
Fax 889-3193

Period furnishings and large rooms give this dignified hotel a comfortable atmosphere. 150 rooms.

Hotel Shoreham ||

33 W 55th, NY 10019
Tel. 247-6700/1-800-553-3347
Fax 376-516

Excellent location for shops, museums and top restaurants. Pantry, cable TV. 123 rooms.

St Moritz on the Park |||

50 Central Park South, NY 10019
Tel. 755-5800/1-800-221-4774
Fax 752-5097

Up the block and down the price scale a bit from the Plaza, overlooking Central Park. 692 rooms.

St Regis |||

2 E 55th St, NY 10022
Tel. 753-4500/1-800-750-7550
Fax 688-5948

Recently renovated *grande dame* of Fifth Avenue, furnished with antique reproductions; butler on every floor and amusing Maxfield Parrish mural in the King Cole Bar. Expensive. 322 rooms.

United Nations |||
Plaza Hotel

1 UN Plaza, NY 10017
(First and 2nd on E 44th St)
Tel. 355-3400/1-800-228-9000
Fax 702-5051

Sculptured glass skyscraper opposite the UN. Guest rooms, fitness centre, indoor swimming pool and tennis court. 428 rooms.

The Waldorf-Astoria ▮▮▮
301 Park Ave, NY 10022
(E 49th and 50th Sts)
Tel. 355-3000/1-800-445-8667
Fax 758-9209
New York's most 'royal' hotel includes an elaborate fitness centre, theatre and tour desks, restaurants, shops and bars. 1,408 rooms.

Wyndham Hotel ▮▮
42 W 58th St, NY 10019
(Fifth and Sixth Aves)
Tel. 753-3500/1-800-257-111
Fax 754-5638
Charming, affordable family hotel situated close to Central Park. Old-fashioned rooms. 185 rooms.

EAST SIDE

The Barbizon ▮▮▮
140 E 63rd on Lexington Ave
NY 10021
Tel. 715-6900/1-800-223-1020
Fax 872-7272
Built in the 1920s; conveniently located for Bloomingdale's and the cinemas. 344 rooms.

De Hirsch Residence ▮
1395 Lexington Avenue at
92nd St, NY 10022
Tel. 415-5650/1-800-858-4692
Fax 415-5578
Clean, lowest budget accommodations run by YMHA, appealing to young people. No co-ed rooms. Shared bathrooms. Fitness facility. 295 rooms.

Gramercy Park Hotel ▮▮
2 Lexington Avenue, NY 10010
(at E 21st St)
Tel. 475-4320/1-800-221-4083
Fax 505-0535
Quiet, friendly and quaint old-world residence. 500 rooms.

Hôtel Plaza Athénée ▮▮▮
37 E 64th St, NY 10021
(Park and Madison Aves)
Tel. 734-9100/1-800-447-8800
Fax 772-0958
A European-style hotel boasting French period furnishings; excellent cuisine. 153 rooms.

Hotel Wales ▮▮
1295 Madison Ave, NY 10128
(E 92nd and 93rd St)
Tel. 876-6000/1-800-223-0888
Fax 860-7000
One of the city's oldest hotels, elegantly restored, situated in a residential neighbourhood. 92 rooms.

Hotel Westbury ▮▮▮
Madison Ave at 60th St, NY 10021
Tel. 535-2000
Fax 535-5058
London-style exclusive standby of Upper Eastsiders. Club-like Polo Lounge. 179 rooms, 52 suites.

The Mark ‖‖‖

25 E 77th St, NY 10021
(at Madison Ave)
Tel. 744-4300/1-800-843-6275
Fax 744-2749

This very stylish, comfortable and expensive Upper East Side establishment offers Italian neoclassical suites and 18th-century Piranesi prints. Tea is served in the afternoon. 180 rooms.

The Stanhope ‖‖‖

995 5th Ave near 81st St
NY 10021
Tel. 288-5800/1-800-828-1123
Fax 517-0088

Fairly small hotel, mostly offering suites. An elegant address featuring a classic décor and stylish service. Situated across the avenue from the Metropolitan Museum. Limousine service to opera and theatres. 141 rooms.

FINANCIAL DISTRICT

The Hotel Millenium ‖‖‖

55 Church St, NY 10007
(opposite the World Trade Center)
Tel. 693-2001/1-800-835-2220
Fax 571-2316

Black glass luxury hotel facing the World Trade Center and situated near the shady St Paul's colonial churchyard. Every known amenity. 546 rooms.

GREENWICH VILLAGE

Washington Square Hotel ‖

103 Waverly Place, NY 10011
(McDougal St and Sixth Ave)
Tel. 777-9515/1-800-222-0418
Fax 979-8373

Attractively restored 1902 hotel located in the heart of Greenwich Village. 200 rooms, some with shared bathrooms.

SOHO

Holiday Inn Downtown ‖‖

138 Lafayette St, NY 10013
Tel. 966-8898/1-800-282-3933
Fax 966-3933

Cheaper than the Midtown branch, this hotel, central to SoHo, is a remodelled period building with large, high-ceilinged rooms. European touches. 227 rooms.

WEST SIDE

Aberdeen Hotel ‖

17 W 32nd St, NY 10001
Tel. 736-1600/1-800-826-4667
Fax 695-1813

The Aberdeen is a well-managed, conveniently located budget hotel near Macy's, Madison Square Garden and the Empire State Building. 175 rooms.

71

The Chelsea Inn
46 W 17th St, NY 10011
Tel. 645-8989/1-800-777-8215
Fax 989-3307
Not to be confused with the Hotel Chelsea, this affordable converted townhouse is a find. 13 rooms and seven four-person suites.

Herald Square Hotel
19 W 31st St, NY 10001
(at Fifth Ave)
Tel. 279-4017/1-800-727-1888
Fax 643-9208
This restored 19th-century home of *Life* magazine is near the Empire State Building. 120 rooms, some with shared bathrooms.

Hotel Esplanade
305 West End Ave, NY 10023
(at W 74th St)
Tel. 874-5000/1-800-367-1763
Fax 496-0367
Landmark building near Lincoln Center. Very spacious rooms, some overlooking the river. Reasonable rates. Health club. 120 rooms.

International House
500 Riverside Dr, NY 10027
Tel. 316-8438
Fax 316-1827
Dormitory and 'guest suites' at rock bottom prices for university students, visiting scholars and others, close to Columbia University.

Malibu Studios Hotel
2688 Broadway, NY 10025
(W 102nd and 103rd Sts)
Tel. 222-2954
Fax 678-6842
Budget lodgings on the Upper West Side. 150 studios, some units with private bathrooms.

The Mayflower Hotel
15 Central Park West, NY 10023
(W 61st and 62nd Sts)
Tel. 265-0060/1-800-223-4164
Fax 265-5098
An old-world hotel, rooms overlooking Central Park. 371 rooms.

New York International American Youth Hostel
891 Amsterdam Ave at
W 103rd St, NY 10025
Tel. 932-3200
Fax 932-2574
New York's only member of the International Youth Hostel system (see p.139). Garden, cafeteria, kitchen and laundry. Lowest rates. 480 beds, in four to 12-bed dormitory rooms; singles available.

Riverside Tower Hotel
80 Riverside Dr, NY 10024
Tel. 877-5200/1-800-724-3136
Fax 873-1400
Budget hotel with kitchenettes in residential area overlooking the park and Hudson River. 96 rooms.

Recommended Restaurants

To give a rough guide to the price of eating out in New York, restaurants are categorized by the approximate cost of a three-course à la carte dinner for one person, excluding drinks, tax and tips. Many establishments serve reasonably priced 'prix fixe' and pre-theatre dinners, as well as weekend brunches. Reservations are recommended.

‖‖	above $35
‖	$15-35
‖	below $15

MIDTOWN

Akbar ‖
475 Park Ave
(E 57th and 58th Sts)
Tel. 838-1717
Authentic North Indian cuisine in a bright, sky-lit room. Good tandoori chicken and chicken ginger kebab. Vegetarian specialities available. Also at 256 E 49th St (tel. 755-9100).

American Festival Café ‖
Rockefeller Center, 20 W 50th St
(Fifth and Sixth Aves)
Tel. 246-6699
American. Overlooking the famous skating rink, the Café takes over the Lower Plaza in summer with pink umbrellas, geraniums and a fountain lit in pastel colours. Specialities: cold poached salmon, Maryland crab cakes, prime rib.

Aquavit ‖‖‖
13 W 54th St
(Fifth and Sixth Aves)
Tel. 307-7311
Scandinavian. Set in a sensational two-tiered atrium (the upper-floor café is less expensive than the restaurant downstairs), this refined restaurant offers marinated salmon, smorgasbord platters, smoked Arctic venison, and several herb-flavoured aquavits. Closed Saturday lunchtime and Sunday.

Benihana of Tokyo ‖
47 W 56th St, also 120 E 56th St
(between Park & Lexington)
Tel. 561-09369 (West) and
593-1627 (East)
Dexterous showmanship and impressive swordplay are in order, as Japanese chefs at your grill-topped table slice and cook your order with a magician's speed – it's fun.

73

Billy's ||
948 1st Ave near 52nd St
Tel. 753-1870
Founded in 1870 when stockyards weren't far away, this family-owned no-frills establishment offers honest drinks, good steak tartare and several other solid fare to grateful WASPs from nearby Sutton Place.

La Bonne Soupe |
48 W 55th St
(Fifth and Sixth Aves)
Tel. 608-3852
Hearty soups served with salad, bread, dessert and drink in atmospheric French midtown bistro. La Bonne Soupe also serves egg, fish and meat dishes.

Broadway Diner |
1726 Broadway (at W 55th St)
Tel. 765-0909
A white-tiled 1950s-style diner dishing out huge portions.

Cabana Carioca ||
123 W 45th St
(Sixth and Seventh Aves)
Tel. 581-8088
Brazilian. This restaurant is a popular Theater District dining spot, serving huge portions of *mariscada* seafood stew and *feijoada*, a tangy, salty stew composed of black beans, meat and sausage.

Carnegie Delicatessen & Restaurant |
854 Seventh Ave (at W 55th St)
Tel. 757-2245
Legendary delicatessen serving pastrami (seasoned smoked beef), delicious corned-beef sandwiches and numerous other specialities.

21 Club |||
21 W 52nd St
Tel. 582-7200
Maybe New York's most famous restaurant because of the business celebrities who have charge accounts here. A 'speakeasy' during Prohibition, it has a great bar and warm ambiance.

La Côte Basque |||
5 E 55th St
Tel. 688-6525
This beautiful room is a favourite with New York's 'beautiful people'. Superb French cuisine. Reservation recommended.

The Four Seasons |||
99 E 52nd St
(Park and Lexington Aves)
Tel. 754-9494
Continental/international. In the landmark Seagram Building, the Four Seasons is rated a culinary institution. Try the Grill Room for lunch – crab cakes, grilled fish and meat – and the Pool Room for

dinner – ragout of lobster, crisp farmhouse duck, game in season. Grill Room and Pool Room closed Saturday lunchtime and Sunday.

Hard Rock Café ▯▯
221 W 57th St
between Broadway and 7th Ave
Tel. 459-9320
A Cadillac embedded over the entrance and throng of tourists marks this popular bar and fast food den where the famous T-shirts originate. Deafening music.

Joe Allen ▯▯
326 W 46th St
Tel. 581-6464
This is the place for good hamburgers and quick service en route to the theatre or afterwards. A long-time favourite of show folk.

The Manhattan Ocean Club ▯▯▯
57 W 58th St
(Fifth and Sixth Aves)
Tel. 371-7777
American. An excellent seafood restaurant, the two-tiered Manhattan Ocean Club, adorned with numerous Picasso plates and paintings, specializes in baked oysters and clams, juicy grilled swordfish, salmon steak and spicy crab cakes. The Club is closed Saturday and Sunday lunchtime.

Nanni ▯▯
146 E 46th St
Tel. 697-4161
Excellent, long-established North Italian trattoria famed for its absolutely perfect 'angel's hair' pasta. Simple surroundings.

Nirvana ▯▯▯
30 Central Park South
Tel. 486-5700
This establishment serves tandoori specialities in an Indian/Bangladeshi décor on a rooftop with a sensational view.

The Oak Room and Bar ▯▯▯
The Plaza Hotel
Fifth Ave and 59th St
Tel. 546-5330
A comfortable and pleasant wood-panelled world with English overtones. Fine old bar and traditional dishes on the menu.

Oyster Bar & Restaurant ▯▯
Grand Central Terminal,
lower level
(E 42nd St at Vanderbilt Ave)
Tel. 490-6650
American. A vast dining hall that offers juicy oysters, fresh fish and tasty shellfish stews and chowders (hearty seafood soups). Closed Saturday and Sunday.

75

The Rainbow Room   ▮▮▮

30 Rockefeller Plaza
(W 49th and 50th Sts)
Tel. 632-5000
Continental. Located on the 65th floor of the RCA Building, the city's most fashionable supper club serves up dishes such as oysters Rockefeller, lobster thermidor and tournedos Rossini. Dinner only. Closed Monday.

The Russian Tea Room   ▮▮▮

150 W 57th St west of Sixth Ave
Tel. 265-0947
Many musicians, agents, theatre folk and Carnegie Hall concert-goers make this renowned *shashlik*, vodka and caviar emporium their watering hole. A very special place. Reserve.

Shun Lee Palace   ▮▮

155 E. 55th St
Tel. 371-8844
A very fine menu at prices reflecting the upscale neighbourhood, but good value for a group sharing from a vast array of delicacies.

Smith and Wollensky   ▮▮▮

201 E 49th St at Third Ave
Tel. 753-1530
A great place for a taste of American steaks, chops and lobsters – New Yorkers give this macho retreat top ranking.

Sushiden   ▮▮

19 E 49th St
(Madison Ave)
Tel. 758-27000
Japanese. *Sushi* and *sashimi* specialities served at tables or counters of Japanese cypress. Hot dishes available as well.

Symphony Café   ▮▮

950 Eighth Ave
(at W 56th St)
Tel. 397-9595
American. This handsome and casual café serves a fine cuisine of home-made pasta, salmon steaks, roasted duckling.

EAST SIDE

PJ Clarke's   ▮▮

915 3rd Ave
Tel. 759-1650
PJ's is a classified historical landmark, so they can't tear down this little brick building surrounded by mighty towers. The crowded old-time bar and dark back room are for meeting as much as eating.

Condon's   ▮▮

117 E 15th St
(Union Sq. East and Irving Pl)
Tel. 254-0960
American. An intimate grotto for good bistro food (Maryland crab cakes) and live jazz. Garden.

Les Halles ▌▌

411 Park Ave South
(E 28th and 29th Sts)
Tel. 679-4111
French. A genuine Parisian bistro
right in the heart of Manhattan.
Les Halles specializes in delicious
charcuterie platters, *cassoulets* and
steak tartare.

Serendipity 3 ▌

225 E 60th St
(Second and Third Aves)
Tel. 838-3531
In this unusual toy shop/restaurant
you will be offered foot-long hot
dogs, burgers, tiny pizzas and hot
fudge sundaes.

Shaliga Thai Cuisine ▌▌

834 Second Ave near 44th St
Tel. 573-5526
Thais create imaginative mixtures,
both spicy and mild, that surprise
and delight. This restaurant is a
small, unpretentious spot popular
with UN crowd.

The Sign of the ▌▌-▌▌▌
Dove

1110 Third Ave at 65th St
Tel. 861-8080
A veritable stage set – with intimate restaurant, café and sidewalk
bistro – the original Sign of the
Dove serves a light and delicious
creative cuisine.

FINANCIAL DISTRICT

Windows on ▌▌▌
the World

1 World Trade Center
Tel. 938-1111
Continental fare. Windows on the
World offers an unforgettable ex-
perience: you can have a meal
some 107 floors above Manhattan.
The view from the 'City Lights'
bar is great, too.

World Trade Center ▌
Plaza

Under the World Trade Center
Ten Lower Manhattan restaurants,
cafés and bistros have joined
forces to offer a cafeteria presenta-
tion of their specialities in a large
room and outdoor dining area
under the twin towers. The Plaza
is opened Monday to Friday from
11am to 3pm.

SOUTH STREET
SEAPORT

Sweets ▌▌

2 Fulton St
Tel. 825-9786
This long-established restaurant
has been serving fish from the old
Fulton Fish Market since 1842.
An upstairs landmark in the South
Street Seaport area, it is closed
Saturday and Sunday.

77

LOWER EAST SIDE

Ratner's   I
138 Delancey St
Tel. 677-5588
Classic kosher dairy restaurant located in the Lower East Side of Manhattan; it was made famous by all the immigrants who worked their way out of the neighbourhood and return to reminisce over chicken soup with *matzo* balls.

CHINATOWN

Golden Unicorn   II
18 . Broadway
(at Catherine St)
Tel. 941-0911
Chinese. A lively Hong Kong-style restaurant, some say Chinatown's best. Try a plate of *dim sum* (filled dumplings and other food in bite-size portions) or other mouth-watering specialities.

LITTLE ITALY

Angelo's   II
146 Mulberry St
(between Hester and Grand Sts)
Tel. 966-1277
Located in Little Italy, Angelo's offers an authentic bit of Neapolitan chaos. This long-established restaurant has been serving pasta since the turn of the century.

GREENWICH VILLAGE

Benny's Burritos   I
113 Greenwich Ave
(at Jane St)
Tel. 727-0584
Californian and Mexican. Try their specialities, the *burritos* (steamed flour tortillas) served with fresh fillings (lamb, turkey or vegetarian) and wash them down with margaritas in a rowdy village bar atmosphere.

The Coach House   III
110 Waverly Place
Tel. 777-0303
Headed by a respected cookbook writer, the famous Coach House earned a deserved reputation for its list of delicious American and Southern dishes. You'll enjoy the good service and the refined and calm setting. Rather expensive for Greenwich Village.

Elephant & Castle   I
68 Greenwich Ave
(near Seventh Ave)
Tel. 243-1400
American. A Village café famous for its mouth-watering juicy burgers, fluffy omelettes and good salads and desserts. The Elephant & Castle has another branch situated in SoHo at 183 Prince Street (tel. 260-3600).

Gotham Bar & Grill |||

12 E 12th St
(Fifth Ave and University Pl)
Tel. 620-4020

American. A vast, strikingly designed Greenwich Village establishment famous for its *haute cuisine*: seafood salads, subtle fish dishes (tuna, bass), smoked duck, herb-and-mustard basted rack of lamb. Closed Saturday and Sunday lunchtime.

John's Pizza |

278 Bleecker St
(at Seventh Ave)
Tel. 243-1680

Located in Greenwich Village, John's Pizza probably serves the best pizzas in New York.

Minetta Tavern |

113 McDougal St off Bleecker St
Tel. 475-3850

This tavern is worth a visit for its authentic Village bar atmosphere of yesteryear, more than for its average Italian kitchen.

Sevilla ||

62 Charles St
(Seventh Ave and W 4th St)
Tel. 929-3189

Spanish. Situated in the Village, this rustic room filled with Spanish music features fabulous paellas and fruity sangria.

SOHO

Brother's Bar-B-Que |

228 W Houston St
(near Varick St)
Tel. 727-2775

All-American fare. Brother's Bar-B-Que, a SoHo diner resounding with soul music, serves tasty barbecued chicken, hearty ribs and beef brisket.

The Manhattan Brewing Company ||

42 Thompson St,
NY 10013
Tel. 925-1515

Gleaming, bulbous copper vats soar over this stripped-clean but still active brewery, where six of the beers brewed locally are served alongside good fish and chips and several other tasty dishes, including the unusual and delicious malt ice cream.

SoHo Kitchen and Bar ||

103 Greene St
(Spring and Prince Sts)
Tel. 925-1866

American. Simple and hearty fare. Pizzas, pastas, grilled fish, fresh salads, juicy burgers and more than 100 varieties of wine are offered by the glass in this casual SoHo eatery decorated with several art pieces. (Some 15 draught **79** beers can also be sampled.) The high-ceilinged bare-brick vault is built to absorb conversation.

TRIBECA

Bouley ▯▯▯

165 Duane St
(Hudson and Greenwich Sts)
Tel. 608-3852
French. Superb Provençal cuisine served in a very pretty restaurant located in TriBeCa. The menu includes numerous mouth-watering dishes such as lobster, grilled or in a delicious red-wine sauce, braised or roasted pigeon, sautéed scallops and fruity soufflés. Look out for the 'prix fixe' lunch and dinner menus. The restaurant is closed on Saturday lunchtime and Sunday.

WEST SIDE

Café des Artistes ▯▯▯

1 W 67th St
Tel. 877-3500
Delicious and authentic French cuisine (and weekend brunch) in charming rooms within a hotel off Central Park. (The building was created in 1913 to house artists and their studios.) Succulent desserts and lively atmosphere are just two of its characteristics. Has a 'prix fixe' lunch. Close to Lincoln **80** Center. Reserve!

The Ginger Man ▯▯

51 W 64th St
Tel. 874-5100
A warm pub atmosphere and a young crowd make this restaurant a lively spot at weekends. An excellent address for simple pre-concert and theatre dining.

Pasta Pot ▯

160 Eighth Ave
(at W 18th St)
Tel. 633-9800
Authentic and inviting Italian eatery situated in the heart of Chelsea, featuring some 20 different kinds of pasta.

Shun Lee West ▯

43 W 65th St
Tel. 595-8895
This West Side cousin of the Shun Lee Palace (see p.76) is a popular venue for its Szechuan dishes.

Tavern on the Green ▯▯-▯▯▯

67th St and Central Park West
Tel. 873-3200
Everybody's favourite in the summer for brunch and outdoor dining in the Park under light-spangled trees. In winter, the sparkles are in the Crystal Room. Handy to Lincoln Center. Rather expensive, but fixed-price lunches and pre-theatre dinners are available.

MUSEUM HIGHLIGHTS

American Museum of Natural History, *Central Park West at West 79th Street*. This is the largest natural history museum in the world; exhibits include human evolution, dinosaurs, gems and a treasury of primitive art. Open Sun-Thurs 10am-5.45pm; Fri-Sat 10am-8.45pm. Suggested admission fee: $5 adults, $2.50 children. (See p.63)

Ellis Island Immigration Museum, *Statue of Liberty ferry from Battery Park*. Permanent and changing exhibitions retrace the sufferings and joys of some 12 million immigrants who entered the US between 1892 and 1924. Admission is free, but the ferry to reach the museum (and the Statue of Liberty) is $6 adults, $3 children. Ferries leave from Battery Park every day between 9.30am and 3.30pm. (See p.90)

The Metropolitan Museum of Art, *Fifth Avenue at East 82nd Street*. This treasure house has countless paintings, drawings, prints, musical instruments, furniture and sculpture from all eras and all points of the globe on display in its 250 rooms – a magnificent collection of collections assembling the best from every civilization. Open Sun, Tues, Wed, Thurs 9.30am-5.15pm; Fri, Sat 9.30am-8.45pm. Suggested admission fee: $6 adults, $3 students, children under 12 free. (See p.64)

The Museum of Modern Art, *West 53rd Street between Fifth and Sixth Avenues*. The MOMA houses a superb collection of more than 70,000 works of art from 1880 to the present day – don't miss the cool garden and imposing sculptures. Open Sat-Wed 11am-6pm; Thurs 12-8.30pm. Admission fee: $7.50 adults, $4.50 students. (See p.83)

Whitney Museum of American Art, *Madison Avenue at East 75th Street*. The Whitney is devoted to 20th-century American art, displayed in both permanent and changing exhibitions, and concentrates on the work of living artists. Open Wed, Fri-Sun 11am-6pm, Thurs 1-8pm. Admission fee: $6 adults, $5 students and seniors, Thurs 6-8pm free. (See p.85)

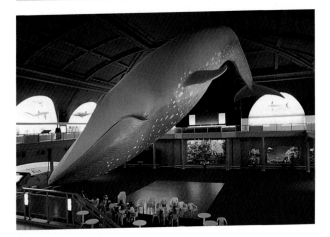

No visitor, foreign or native, should miss the unique American Wing, for no other museum in the world can – or has even tried to – match this.

Room after room reflects America's progression from a frugal frontier, with nearly everything hand-made, to affluence and taste. You can climb the majestic wrought-iron and bronze staircase designed by Louis Sullivan for the late 19th-century Chicago Stock Exchange (now demolished) or a superbly carved wooden stair-

The awesome Blue Whale weighs 100 tons – but this one is made of fiberglass.

case from a New Hampshire house of 1700. Furniture is displayed in period rooms partially lit by Tiffany glass windows. All those who think of American painting in mid-20th century terms may be surprised by the superb canvases of Winslow Homer, the grand portraits by Whistler and Sargent, and the disturbing realism of Edward Hopper.

Another wing shelters the magnificent **Temple of Dendur**, brought from the banks of the Nile to be reassembled here stone by stone. The temple was a gift from Egypt in gratitude for help in saving the Abu Simbel Temple from the waters of the Aswan Dam.

Another striking setting, at the west end of the main floor, the **Lehman Collection** presents the donor's fine early Italian and French Impressionist paintings in the original, elegantly furnished décor of his home. The **Michael C Rockefeller Wing** houses a superb collection of primitive art in a spacious, greenhouse-like hall.

The Met's exhibits of European Paintings, Sculpture and Decorative Arts are splendid. See Botticelli's *Last Communion of St Jerome*, Van Gogh's *Cypresses*, Rembrandt's self-portrait, aged 54, or works by El Greco and Goya.

The most delightful touch in the Museum Restaurant, characteristic of the Metropolitan's eclectic and bold display technique, is Jean Dupas's mural in glass, gold and silver leaf, rescued from the French *Normandie* ocean liner, depicting the history of navigation.

And the Met keeps growing: the **20th-Century Wing**, nearly as big as the entire Museum of Modern Art, opened to acclaim in 1987. Featured here are paintings, sculpture and the decorative arts from Europe and America. In the 20th-century room, Americans Pollock, Kline and de Kooning shine. Modern sculpture is on view in the roof garden overlooking Central Park. There's a reasonably priced shop.

The Museum of Modern Art

The MOMA, as it is affectionately known, is devoted to works of art from 1880 to the present day. The size of its collection of more than 70,000 works makes possible important special exhibitions and the rotation of what's on display. Do not miss the garden – in summer it's a cool haven and **83**

the setting for sculptures by Renoir, Picasso, Rodin, Calder, Moore and Maillol. Next to the garden, glass-enclosed escalators lead into the MOMA.

Temporary exhibitions and recent acquisitions appear on the ground floor of the west wing, and there's a kind of 'Hit Parade' room at the top of the first escalator. The display re-cently boasted Matisse's *Dancers*, Rousseau's *Sleeping Gypsy*, Picasso's *Woman Before a Mirror*, Van Gogh's poignant *Starry Night* and a Cézanne *Bather*. And this is just to whet your appetite for the masterpieces in store for you.

MOMA lays claim to some great pieces of **sculpture**, notably Alberto Giacometti's *The*

*F*orm follows function at MOMA's modernist retail shop, where high-quality shopping opportunities abound.

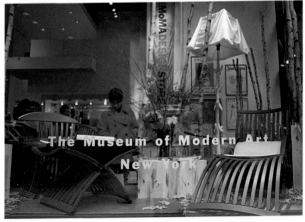

Palace at 4am and Duchamp's *Bicycle Wheel*. There's a prodigious photography collection and a section devoted to architecture and design, with excellence judged by the way 'form follows function', here exemplified by objects ranging from a Wedgwood cup and saucer to a Bang & Olufsen 'Beogram 4002' turntable.

The museum screens classic **films** from its archives every afternoon. No extra admission is charged, but ask for tickets when you pay your entrance fee (tel. 708-9490 for details). Concerts are held in the garden on summer evenings.

Whitney Museum of American Art

The Whitney, devoted to 20th-century American art, concentrates on the works of living artists in both permanent and changing exhibitions; also included are contemporary film and video productions. A museum branch is located at Philip Morris, Park Avenue at East 42nd Street (a sculpture court and gallery).

OTHER ART AND HISTORY MUSEUMS

Abigail Adams Smith Museum: a 1799 landmark house featuring rooms furnished in the Federal and Empire styles. Frequent lectures and concerts (tel. 838-6878 for details).

American Craft Museum: consider the relationship between function and decoration as you look over the very best in American crafts, ranging from old-fashioned rockers to seatless chairs.

Asia Society: fine collection of Oriental arts on display, with changing exhibits and accompanying lectures.

The Children's Museum of Manhattan: 'Go ahead and touch!' replaces 'Don't Touch' at this interactive fun house where children can paint, operate a TV camera and admire the 'Great Stuff!' exhibition, a collection of objects that only kids would call 'collectibles'. There's also a play garden for pre-schoolers.

85

The Cloisters: these genuine cloisters and parts of Middle Ages buildings were brought from France, Italy and Spain and reassembled in Fort Tryon Park. There are some lovely things, including the chapel of San Martín de Fuentiña, all the way from Segovia, the Romanesque cloister of St Michel-de-Cuxa from the Pyrenees, the exquisite Hunt of the Unicorn tapestries and famous Mérode triptych. The peaceful, isolated setting adds to the enjoyment; the garden is fragrant with medicinal herbs used in the Middle Ages. A ride on the M4 bus from Madison Avenue will give you interesting glimpses of Harlem and Washington Heights, though the A train up 8th Avenue to 190th Street is a good deal faster.

Cooper-Hewitt Museum: located in the sumptuous mansion built for Andrew Carnegie in 1900, it owns one of the largest collections of decorative art in the US, from fashions to furniture. Fascinating!

The New York School

The New York art scene was invigorated when émigré artists from Europe arrived shortly before World War II. Members of the avant-garde, these painters made an immediate impact on the cultural life of the city, hastening the development of America's first truly innovative school of painting, the New York school of abstract expressionists.

The key figure of the school was JACKSON POLLOCK, who pioneered the technique of action painting. He applied colour to the canvas in a series of splashes and dribbles, leaving composition to chance. WILLEM DE KOONING followed suit, though sometimes a recognizable subject emerges in his work. Another leading member of the school was FRANZ KLINE, famous for his abstract canvases in black, white and grey.

The Frick Collection: Henry Clay Frick, of Swiss origin, was a steel magnate who, like other American millionaires of the early 20th century, set aside part of his fortune for acquiring works of art. The museum used to be his home, so you can get some idea of the way rich New Yorkers lived.

You can see an 18th-century boudoir with eight panels commissioned from François Boucher by Madame de Pompadour, a Fragonard salon containing an assortment of fine pieces and a dining room with portraits by Hogarth, Reynolds and Gainsborough. Other treasures include El Greco's *St Jerome as Cardinal*, Holbein portraits, *Philip II of Spain* by Velázquez, *Education of the Virgin* by de La Tour, a lovely Vermeer, Giorgione Bellini's *St. Francis*, some striking full-length portraits by Whistler and three Rembrandts, including the disputed but handsome *Polish Rider*. The furniture and exhibits are priceless.

Chamber music concerts are occasionally held in one of the most charming areas of the museum, the glass-domed, marble-floored courtyard with its pool and fountain.

Solomon R Guggenheim Museum: the 1959 building, by Frank Lloyd Wright, is still as modern as tomorrow, fitting as a gallery for modern artists. The recent expansion by construction of a tower in Wright's original plans and the addition of interior galleries have doubled the Guggenheim's space. Changing exhibitions are hung on the walls of a ramp that winds up six storeys around a central well.

The basic collection is that of Solomon Guggenheim, who came to the US from Switzerland and made his fortune in copper. His collection is noted for works by Kandinsky, Klee, Calder and Chagall. The Justin K Thannhauser collection, in an annex, contains paintings by Renoir, Monet, Cézanne, Van Gogh, Gauguin and Degas. The museum's café is run by Dean & DeLuca – esteemed caterers.

In 1992 a SoHo branch of the Guggenheim opened at Broadway and Prince Street to show **87** some of the permanent collection and offer space to new, modern works of art.

International Center of Photography: another Fifth Avenue mansion turned museum, the ICP showcases the work of outstanding photographers; the bookstore there is the best of its kind in the city.

The Intrepid Sea-Air-Space Museum: the *Intrepid* is a decommissioned US Navy aircraft carrier packed with exhibits about sea exploration and warfare, space travel and aviation. On deck, dozens of aircrafts include the world's fastest, the spy plane *Blackbird*; beside it, explore a submarine; on land, inspect Iraqi armoured vehicles captured in the Gulf War.

The Jewish Museum: recently renovated, the museum holds an extensive collection of Judaica and exhibits the work of Jewish artists.

Museum of the City of New York: kids will love the doll's houses and pre-plastic toys exhibited in the Toy Gallery. Adults, meanwhile, will get a better idea of what 'little old New York' was like from photos, models and dioramas.

SCIENCE AND THEME MUSEUMS

Museum of Television and Radio: in addition to uninterrupted screenings of all-time favourite shows of both media, visitors can request specific episodes out of the 50,000 items in the archives. Special programmes for children.

The National Museum of the American Indian, Smithsonian Institution. *At the same address: Hispanic Society of America; and the American Numismatic Society.*
Recently, these once hard-to-find museums moved to the former US Customs House at

'Top guns' discuss the merits of the Corsair fighter aboard the aircraft carrier Intrepid.

Bowling Green, at the foot of Manhattan. They were open to the public in October 1994. The Indian collection can at last be seen in a proper gallery. The Hispanic Society's gallery holds surprises – paintings by Goya, El Greco and Veláz- quez. Surely no coin collector will want to miss the exhibi- tion of coins on display at the Numismatic Society, Ameri- ca's most extensive.

Pierpont Morgan Library: rare books, illuminated manu- scripts, Florentine sculpture, Old Master paintings, etc, all amassed by the American banker J Pierpont Morgan.

The New Museum of Con- temporary Art: 'contempo- rary' at this SoHo institution means not more than 10 years old, and also 'far out'.

South Street Seaport Historic District: this restored seaport area of 19th-century buildings and sailing ships has a Chil- dren's Center museum, an ex- hibit of model ships and an art gallery (see pp.43-5).

Excursions

THE STATUE OF LIBERTY AND ELLIS ISLAND

Take the ferry to the statue from Battery Park, the southern tip of Manhattan (tickets are av- ailable at Clinton Castle). Dai- ly 15-minute crossings depart every 30 minutes from 9.30am to 3.30pm, Adults pay $6, chil- dren $3. The sights are open daily from 9am to 5pm; allow at least two hours' sightseeing on each island. For further in- formation call 363-3200.

The **Statue of Liberty** is the most recognized symbol of the United States, known all over the world. The statue, some ten years in the making, was a gift from France in recognition of the friendship between the two countries; it was to serve as a beacon for immigrants arriv- ing in the New World.

Frédéric-Auguste Bartholdi's 151ft (46m) structure is one of those wild dreams that become reality. Engineering expertise had to be harnessed to art, so Bartholdi called in Gustave Eiffel – of Eiffel Tower fame – to help translate his vision into metal. Skilled workmen in the French capital erected the statue in 1884, as bemused Parisians watched her crowned head rise above their rooftops. It was later dismantled and shipped in 214 huge wooden crates for reassembly on Liberty Island. The statue of 'Liberty Enlightening the World' was officially unveiled by President Cleveland on 28 October 1886.

Once ashore, head for the elevator to the promenade at the top of the 89ft (27m) high base of the statue. You should expect at least an hour's wait, but the spectacular **views** of the Manhattan skyline are worth every minute. In order to reach the lady's crown, you'll have to climb a 22-storey staircase. If you don't make the climb, take a look at the video of the view is shown below. Exhibits picture the statue's history.

After your visit, catch the next ferry on to **Ellis Island**. The Ellis Island Immigration Museum on the islet just north of the Statue of Liberty opened in the Main Building in 1990.

It retraces, through a touching introductory film, audio-visual displays and permanent and changing exhibitions, the sufferings and joys of some 12 million immigrants who entered the US through these doors between 1892 and 1924, when consulates abroad took over the screening process.

The transatlantic steamers anchored at Quarantine in the New York Narrows. First- and second-class passengers were inspected aboard and landed in New York with American citizens. 'Steerage'-class passengers (who had paid an average $30 to travel in unspeakable conditions) were unloaded onto barges for Ellis Island, where the anxious immigrants would troop up flights of stairs to the Great Hall to undergo medical scrutiny and face a barrage of questions. Their future depended on making it through this examination – a human drama re-enacted millions of times.

Corrupt officials and money changers sometimes swindled families out of even the few dollars they possessed until the service was reformed in 1901. **91**

Among those who made it were actors Claudette Colbert, Bob Hope and Edward G Robinson, composer Irving Berlin, the Von Trapp family of *The Sound of Music* fame and poet Khalil Gibran.

BOAT AND HELICOPTER TRIPS

Splendid views of the city are in store when you take one of a variety of **boat trips** around Manhattan. For example, from March to December, the **Circle Line** (tel. 563-3200) leaves from Pier 83 at the foot of West 43rd Street at Twelfth Avenue for a three-hour-long, 35-mile (56km) cruise around Manhattan – you may choose to combine this outing with a visit to the *Intrepid*, the museum ship docked at Pier 86 (see p.88).

If your time is limited, the Seaport **Harbor Cruise Line** operates a 90-minute excursion of Lower Manhattan and the Statue of Liberty aboard a replica paddlewheel steamer leaving from South Street Seaport. A guide indicates points of interest: architectural, historic,

cultural or simply anecdotal; tel. 385-0791 for details.

You can also see Manhattan in 75-minute cruises from a **catamaran**, which leaves from Pier 11, near the bottom of Wall Street. The sleek **Spirit of New York** operates lunch and dinner cruises with narration and music from the adjacent Pier 9; tel. 742-7278 for reservations. **World Yacht** organizes lunch, brunch and dinner cruises with live music for dancing from Pier 81 at West 41st Street, tel. 630-8100 for information.

The **ferry** from Battery Park to the Statue of Liberty and Ellis Island operates year-round. The last outbound ferry leaves at 3.30pm. The Staten Island Ferry also leaves from Battery Park; it offers impressive views of Manhattan and the Statue of Liberty. Pay on the return.

Flying in a **helicopter** over the skyscraper skyline and the

*B*etween 1892 and 1924, twelve million immigrants passed through Ellis Island.

Statue of Liberty is an unforgettable experience, and a variety of tours is available: the shortest flight lasts only five minutes and doesn't go beyond the United Nations area, while the longest covers the whole town. Flights leave daily, year-round, either from the Heliport on the East River at 34th Street (Island Helicopter Sightseeing, tel. 683-4575) or from the Heliport at the foot of West 30th Street on the Hudson River (Liberty Helicopter Tours, tel. 967-6464). (See also p.129.)

BROOKLYN HEIGHTS

Why not go beyond Manhattan at least once for a visit to Brooklyn? With 2¼ million inhabitants, it has a larger population than Manhattan and is one of the largest urban centres in America. Brooklynites take pride in their accent and traditions, and they don't cross over to Manhattan unless they really have to. Take the subway No. 2 or 3 on Broadway Line as far as Clark Street Station. An interesting way to get

there is on foot via the Brooklyn Bridge from the east side of City Hall Park.

Brooklyn Heights, on the East River, is one of the most attractive areas. The Promenade, three blocks down Clark Street, is an esplanade with one of the most impressive views in the world: at your feet, ships unloading their cargoes of sugar and coffee; in front of you, downtown Manhattan with all its bridges; beyond that, the Bay of New York and the Statue of Liberty. Late afternoon, when the sun is setting, is a good time to go.

At the end of the Promenade, walk south along Hicks Street, a shady street in a quarter that has barely changed since 1860. The brownstone houses (see p.50) are still in fashion and much sought after. When you reach Atlantic Avenue, one of the longest in Brooklyn, you'll find yourself in a Middle Eastern neighbourhood, with Arab restaurants and grocery stores. On Sunday, Atlantic Avenue teems with Americans of Middle Eastern descent who come **94** to do their shopping.

BRONX PARK

For **Bronx Zoo**, take the Seventh Avenue/Broadway No. 2 express subway (or the Lexington Avenue No. 5 train uptown, change to No. 2 train at 180th Street to Pelham Parkway and walk west to the Bronxdale entrance. For more information, call (718) 367-1010.

Bronx zoo is open weekdays from 10am to 5pm; Saturday and Sunday from 10am to 5.30pm; from November to February, it's open daily from 10am to 4.30pm. Adults pay $2.50, children $1 – entrance is free on Wednesday.

Bronx Zoo covers 265 acres (107ha) and shelters more than 4,000 animals and 500 birds, many visible from the guided tour on a monorail train and from the Skyfari aerial tramway. Indoors, don't miss the Jungle World rainforest or the World of Darkness house for viewing nocturnal creatures. For the young ones, there's also a great Children's Zoo, as well as camel rides.

For the **New York Botanical Garden**, take the Avenue of

the Americas D or Lexington Avenue No. 4 train to Bedford Park Boulevard and walk east – phone (718) 817-8705. The Garden is open from Tuesday to Sunday from 10am to 6pm, and in winter Tuesday to Sunday from 10am to 4pm.

The 250-acre (100ha) garden houses 2,700 rose bushes, and the all-glass conservatory, with palms under a 90ft (27m) crystal dome, covers almost an acre. Inside, you will find palm trees and some 5,500 orchids of 650 species.

New York's Best Bridges

New York has 65 bridges, 14 of which connect the island of Manhattan with the surrounding area.

The 1,595ft (486m) **Brooklyn Bridge** created a sensation when it opened in 1883, but it was plagued by misfortune from the start. Its engineer, John Roebling, died in the early phases of the project as a result of an accident, and his son, who carried on the work, was paralyzed by the 'bends' suffered in the course of the job. Tthey were not the only casualties. Nonetheless, the bridge, with its wire webbing, is a great success and a favourite subject for photographers and Sunday painters. The view from the bridge is best at night.

The double-decker **George Washington Bridge** spans the Hudson River between Manhattan and New Jersey. Designed by OH Ammann, its graceful lines show up best at night, when the bridge is illuminated.

Newest on the New York horizon is one of the world's longest suspension structures: measuring 4,260ft (1,298m), the **Verrazano-Narrows Bridge** from Brooklyn to Staten Island is also the work of Ammann. It's named after the Florentine explorer who discovered New York Bay in 1524, landing near the bridge's Staten Island base.

What to Do

Shopping

One of the great joys of New York is window shopping. Just stroll down Fifth Avenue from 59th Street, preferably on a sunny day, and you can't help being dazzled by the fabulous jewellery displays, luxurious leather goods, exquisite crystal and porcelain, discount stores and clothes, clothes, clothes.

There's always some kind of sale going on in New York. The Sunday papers are full of advertisements on current ones, as well as publicity for discount stores specializing in electronic equipment.

What to Buy

Art and antiques: art galleries and antique shops are found throughout the city, with items that range from the exorbitant to the relatively affordable.

*F*or unusual gifts and souvenirs, browse through New York's eclectic markets.

The largest concentration of galleries is situated along East 57th Street and in SoHo. Two institutions worth visiting for their choice are: the Manhattan Art & Antiques Center (Second Avenue between East 55th and 56th Sts), boasting more than a hundred shops and galleries, and the Place des Antiquaires (East 57th St between Park and Lexington Avenues), with 50-odd shops.

Clothing: you really can find bargains among the prodigious array of clothes in the department stores, especially during end-of-season sales. Jeans and cotton clothes in the shops just across Lexington Avenue from Bloomingdale's are generally good buys. Madison Avenue in the East 60s is where it's at for high fashion boutiques, SoHo for more daring designs, Fifth Avenue for reliable labels.

Gadgets: in this paradise for gadget-lovers, you can find an original gift to take home. The best selection appears before Christmas in speciality shops and big stores' household departments. The best is Hammacher-Schlemmer (147 East 57th Street). Hardware stores (do-it-yourself tools and gadgets) are as uniquely comprehensive as the drugstores – and hard to pass up.

Jewellery: the range on offer goes from costume jewellery to elaborate, rather expensive **97**

but original creations, not forgetting the more budget-wise diamond centre on West 47th St and hand-made items, mostly in silver and copper, in Greenwich Village boutiques.

Records, books and videos: choose from a vast selection of the latest releases on disk, tape and CD in classical, rock, folk, jazz and pop music at Tower Records on Broadway at 66th Street near Lincoln Center and at Broadway and West 4th St in Greenwich Village, and at the large HMV on Broadway and 72nd Street.

In the book realm, Barnes & Noble (Fifth Avenue at East 18th Street), one of the world's largest bookshops, offers discounted bestsellers at several midtown branches and a huge new store on the Upper West Side on Broadway at 83rd St. Brentano's, at 597 Fifth Avenue, the Gothman Book Mart, at 41 West 47th Street, and Coliseum Books on Broadway at 57th Street are great places to browse. Among other excellent bookstores are Doubleday Book Shop (the largest branch at Fifth Avenue and West 57th Street, fine art books specialist), Rizzoli (at 31 West 57th St) and the renowned Strand Book Store (Broadway at East 12th Street), the country's largest second-hand book dealer. The museum gift shops are well-stocked with art books.

Sports equipment: Macy's and its rival A&S on West 34th St have wide selections. To join the rollerblade mania, try Blades at 160 East 86th Street. The Fifth Avenue Golf Center near 47th Street stocks 500 different sets of clubs. Ski rentals are available at the Scandinavia Ski and Sport Shop, 40 West 57th Street. You'll find sports equipment shops galore listed in the Yellow Pages telephone directory.

Toys: the ultimate toy store is FAO Schwarz (Fifth Avenue at East 58th Street) where, should you feel like it, a doll's house will be yours to keep for a mere $10,000. Shackman's at Fifth Avenue and 16th Street, is another good place for doll's houses and their furnishings.

When and Where to Shop

Most stores are open Monday to Saturday from 10am to 6pm. Many shops and department stores open at least one night a week, usually on Thursday. All the large department stores are open on Sunday afternoons.

Generally, shops in Greenwich Village, SoHo and Chelsea (shopping concentrated on Seventh Avenue from W 14th to 23rd Streets) are open noon-7 or 8pm, except on Monday.

Department stores: Bloomingdale's (Third Avenue at East 59th Street) is almost a city in itself, a store you should visit for the most up-to-the-minute clothing, furniture (go and see the model rooms), accessories and fine gourmet section. Macy's (West 34th Street at Broadway), known as the largest department store in the world, sells just about everything, and A&S Plaza's eight floors (Avenue of the Americas between 32nd and 33rd Sts) make the very same claim. Why not judge for yourself?

For the latest in fine fashions, saunter down Fifth Avenue from 58th to 39th Streets, stopping on your way at Henri Bendel, Bergdorf Goodman, Saks Fifth Avenue and Lord & Taylor. On Seventh Avenue at West 17th Street, Barney's New York concentrates on men's and women's designer clothes.

Alluring window displays on Fifth Avenue are difficult to ignore. Wait for the sales if you can!

99

It also has several departments for special sizes. A super new branch of Barney's has recently opened at 61st Street and Madison Avenue.

Malls and centres: some of New York City's most prestigious shops occupy premises in Trump Tower (Fifth Avenue at East 56th Street), next door to Tiffany & Co. Further down Fifth Avenue, more than 200 stores fill the underground and street-level shopping complex of Rockefeller Center. At Fifth Avenue and East 47th Street, the fashionable four-level 575 Fifth Avenue mall is crowned by a stained-glass ceiling. The Market at Citicorp Center (see p.36) features three floors of bright, lively and varied shops.

In downtown Manhattan the SoHo Emporium (West Broadway between Spring Street and Broome Street) houses some 40 chic shops under a Civil War-period roof, and in the Financial District the myriad stores and boutiques housed in the World Trade Center and World Financial Center cater to a **100** multitude of tastes.

An interesting open-air flea market is held on Saturday and Sunday on Avenue of the Americas between 24th and 26th Streets. Another Antiques and Collectibles Fair takes place in trendy SoHo at Broadway and Grand Street.

Entertainment

When the sun goes down and the theatre signs light up, New York starts moving to another rhythm. A quick tour of the city's nightlife might include some of the following: a brash, exuberant Broadway musical; a dark, smoke-filled club throbbing to a saxophone's wail; a long line of people waiting patiently to see a film; elegant first-nighters sipping a glass of champagne at the Met; a tinkling piano playing Gershwin at a 40s-style bar; and the cool frenzy of the dance clubs. But even this list doesn't begin to cover the scene.

To find out what's on, consult the Friday newspapers, the 'Arts & Leisure' section of the *Sunday New York Times* or the weekly publications, *The New Yorker*, *New York Magazine* and *The Village Voice*. For details on obtaining theatre and concert tickets, see p.40.

Theatre

For many people, one of the main reasons for visiting New York is to take in a few shows. Broadway naturally means musicals, comedies and conventional drama, with big stars in elaborate productions. Tickets for hit shows can be very difficult to obtain at short notice, so it's highly recommended to reserve your seats ahead of time if you have your heart set on a particular one. Generally, curtain-up time is 8pm, with matinées on Wednesday, Saturday and sometimes Sunday.

Off-Broadway and Off-Off-Broadway theatres are scattered all over town. Generally smaller, they can be top-flight or amateur affairs; whichever the case, the tickets are invariably cheaper. The plays featured range from revivals of the classics to the most avant-garde theatrical experiments.

To name but one establishment, the Public Theater (425 Lafayette Street), which may have several different kinds of productions going at once, can usually be counted on for an interesting evening.

Dance

When it comes to dance, New York fairly bubbles over with activity: here are the headquarters of modern dance, and classical ballet makes a creditable showing, too. Between the resident companies – New York City Ballet, Merce Cunningham, Alvin Ailey, Dance Theater of Harlem and the American Ballet Theater – and up-and-coming groups like Plath/Taucher, dance fans are really spoiled for choice.

Opera and Concert

New York City's two major opera companies occupy adjoining buildings in the Lincoln Center. The Met may have the glamour and the Italian tenors but the New York City Opera can lay claim to a more modern **101** and adventurous repertory. In any case, they're both superb. As for concerts of classical music, you're likely to find a dozen or so scheduled for a single evening – with the New York Philharmonic (also at Lincoln Center) heading the bill.

Renowned for its excellent acoustics, Carnegie Hall plays host to outstanding visiting artists. Free concerts are held frequently in the Bruno Walter Auditorium of the New York Public Library at Lincoln Center. In the summer, the Met and the Philharmonic give free performances in the city's parks.

Movie Theatres

Every New York neighbourhood has its movie theatres, but the two largest concentrations are in the Times Square area and along Third Avenue above East 57th Street, and they feature the newest films and the highest prices. The Walter Reade Theatre at Lincoln Center and the MOMA specialize in revivals of Hollywood classics and subtitled foreign films, as do several other houses listed in New York's weekly magazines.

The Late-Night Scene

Great jazz clubs featuring all styles – avant-garde, modern and traditional jazz – are found all over the city, but the largest concentration is in the Village (try the Village Vanguard or The Blue Note) and in SoHo. A special Jazzline telephone number, 1-718-465-7500 tells who's playing where.

Shows are presented nightly at most of New York's comedy clubs, some of which gave the nation's top comedians their start. Among other nightlife attractions, you'll find scores of rock, pop, country-western and dance clubs (even 'ballroom', including the good old Roseland on Broadway).

Old-time nightclubs, such as the Copacabana and The Rainbow Room, still pack them in for dining and dancing without the disco din – but be prepared to spend generously. A number of ethnic nightclubs – from Spanish to French and Brazilian – vary the scene.

Sports

New Yorkers are sports-mad, whether actively as joggers and skaters, or emotionally as rabid fans of local teams. In **Central Park** you can hire a bicycle or a boat or a horse (Claremont Stables, 175 West 89th Street, tel. 724-5100). To play tennis there, you'll need a permit for the season (not required for lessons), but there are courts elsewhere in the city (see the Yellow Pages of the telephone directory) for hire by the hour. Otherwise, you can just follow the example of the thousands of New Yorkers who jog in Central Park and along the city pavements. In winter there's ice skating in

*I*ce skates and rollerblades alternate seasonally at the Woolman Memorial Rink in Central Park.

the Park and at Rockefeller Center. Bowlmor Lanes at 110 University Place in Greenwich Village has 44 lanes and tennis courts upstairs.

New York boasts 14 miles (some 23km) of public **beaches**. There are well-tended indoor and outdoor **swimming pools** serving every part of the city, as well as pools at the YMCA and YMHA facilities (see p.116). And if you're really keen on keeping fit during your stay in New York, try joining the Better Bodies Cross-Training Center (tel. 929-6789) at 22 West 19th Street, where you can work out on **weights** and machines and experience the gruelling aerobics Cross Training Facility.

The city's **stadiums**, arenas and courts are stages for world class events. The baseball season runs from April to late September; the football season (American-style) from September to late December. If you want to attend a big game, remember to buy your ticket well in advance. Ask your hotel concierge or go to a Ticketmaster (tel. 307-7171) outlet.

As for less important games, you'll probably be able to get tickets at the gate if you are lucky. Consult the Friday local newspapers (see p.127) for a rundown on the weekend sporting activities.

The **Mets** baseball team can be seen playing at Shea Stadium in Queens, not far from LaGuardia Airport. The No. 7 (Flushing) subway from Grand Central stops right at the stadium. The **Yankees** can be supported at Yankee Stadium in the Bronx (East 161st Street and River Avenue), reached on the No. 4 or D subway. The **Giants** and **Jets** (football) are based at the Meadowlands (Giants Stadium) in northern New Jersey, a vast sports and entertainment complex that also houses the **New Jersey Nets** (basketball) and **Devils** (ice hockey). Thoroughbred, harness or motor racing events also bring the fans out to the Meadowlands.

The important basketball (**New York Knicks**) and ice-hockey (**New York Rangers**) teams play at Madison Square Garden. The Garden is also the place to go to attend world championship boxing, horse shows and various other sporting events.

New Yorkers love to bet on horses – the major race tracks are **Aqueduct** (in Queens) and **Belmont** (in Long Island) – and licensed off-track betting (OTB) establishments are found all over town. The trotters go through their paces at **Roosevelt Raceway** on Long Island, at the **Meadowlands** and at **Yonkers Raceway**. Also on Long Island is the Nassau Coliseum, home to a local ice-hockey team, the Islanders.

Classic among classic New York sports fixtures is the **US Open** Tennis Championships at Flushing Meadows, Queens, in August/September, and the **Virginia Slims** women's tournament, played out in Madison Square Garden in November. In late October or early November, some 23,000 runners participate in the traditional 26½-mile (43km) **New York City Marathon**, which starts on Staten Island and ends hours later in Central Park at the Tavern on the Green.

Children

Children absolutely love New York: there is lots for them to do and endless sights to see. Of course they'll enjoy the skyscrapers, the boat trips, the **Statue of Liberty** and riding atop a tour bus, but there are many activities aimed specifically at kids. First of all, the **American Museum of Natural History** and Hayden Planetarium have got to be at the top of the list. In addition to the regular exhibits, there's a Discovery Room, with hands-on demonstrations and a teacher in charge of the activities. For admission, ask at the Information Desk.

The **Children's Museum** is so popular that it could have been designed by children. Kids will love the dolls' houses and toys on display at the **Museum of the City of New York** and just about everything at the **South Street Seaport** marine complex. Virtually all museums in New York have something for children. (For further details see pages 63-90, and pages 130-2.)

CALENDAR OF EVENTS

Pertinent information on special events can be found in the three daily newspapers (*New York Times, Daily News,* and *The Post*) and in the weekly magazines (*The New Yorker, New York*).

31 December *New Year's celebration,* Times Square.

January *Chinese New Year's Day,* Chinatown. A moveable feast, falling between 21 January and 19 February). The pavements are minefields of firecrackers – noisy but harmless.

March *New York Flower Show,* Pier 92, 51st Street and Hudson River. *Ringling Brothers,* Barnum & Bailey Circus at Madison Square Garden.

17 March *St Patrick's Day Parade,* Fifth Avenue – for some great Irish hospitality.

April *Radio City Music Hall Easter Show. Baseball season* opens, runs into October at Yankee Stadium (Bronx) and Shea Stadium (Queens).

May *Memorial Day,* the last Monday in May, features concerts, a boat festival and fireworks, at South Street Seaport.

June *Lesbian/Gay Pride March* along Fifth Avenue. *Washington Square Outdoor Arts Festival* (early June). *Puerto Rican Day Parade* up Fifth Avenue (mid-June). *Free Metropolitan Opera concerts* in the parks of all five boroughs in June/July.

3-13 June *Feast of Sant'Antonio,* Sullivan Street, Little Italy – street fair with Italian food.

July *Shakespeare-in-the-Park,* free performances nightly, through August too, at the Delacourt Theater.

	Summergarden evening concerts at the Museum of Modern Art, also through to August.
4 July	*Independence Day*; concert and fireworks in Central Park; fireworks over Lower Hudson River.
September	*US Open tennis championships*, Flushing Meadows, Queens. *Feast of San Gennaro*, Mulberry Street, Little Italy – street fair lasting about ten days. Season opens for *Metropolitan Opera* and *New York Philharmonic Orchestra*, Lincoln Center. *Labor Day Parade* up Fifth Avenue.
October	*New York Film Festival*, Lincoln Center. *Columbus Day Parade*, Fifth Avenue – primarily an Italian affair, but the rest of New York turns out to watch. *Horse-racing season* starts at Aqueduct Raceway; *New York Rangers hockey season* begins at Madison Square Garden.
November	*Fall Flower Show*, New York Botanical Garden, Bronx. *Radio City Music Hall Christmas stage show*. *New York City Ballet winter season*, Lincoln Center. *New York Knicks basketball season* opens at Madison Square Garden. *Virginia Slims tennis tournament*, Madison Square Garden. *New York City Marathon*, finish line at Tavern on the Green, Central Park. *Macy's Thanksgiving Day Parade*, Central Park West and 77th Street to Herald Square – *the* parade for kids.
December	Annual *Christmas tree* and baroque crèche, Metropolitan Museum of Art. Annual performances of *The Nutcracker* by the New York City Ballet, Lincoln Center. Holiday store *window displays* on Fifth Avenue, *Christmas tree* at the Rockefeller Center, *lighting effects* along Park Avenue and Empire State Building.

Central Park is the place to let children burn up energy. Take in the zoo, row a boat, see the model boats, fly a kite, ride the Carousel, take a hike with a conservationist from the Belvedere Castle, rent a bike or skates, climb the Alice in Wonderland statue, flip a frisbee, join the joggers, watch lawn bowling and baseball, cheer the puppets in the Swedish Cottage Marionette Theater (in the south-west corner playground), listen to a storyteller at the Hans Christian Andersen statue. Check at the Dairy for announcement and time of events (tel. 794-6565).

On a rainy day you could go and watch classic children's programmes at the **Museum of Television and Radio**. The Guinness World of Records exhibition in the lobby of the Empire State Building will astound youngsters. Boarding a nuclear missile submarine and an aircraft carrier at the Intrepid Sea-Air-Space Museum is an unforgettable experience.

The Bronx Zoo is a sure bet since it can occupy an entire day (see p.94). So is Coney Island, with its Astroland rides and the scary Cyclone rollercoaster, plus marine antics at the nearby aquarium's shows.

Many Broadway and Off-Off Broadway shows are designed or suitable for children, as are the Radio City Music Hall shows and the city's rich musical and dance offerings.

*I*n this Natural History Museum reconstruction, an Allosaurus *(left)* attacks a Barosaurus.

Eating Out

Certain items of information in this section will already be familiar to US residents, but have been included for visitors from overseas.

New Yorkers like dining out, and trading tips about favourite new restaurants is a Manhattan hobby.

Breakfast consists of fruit juice, toast, bagel, butter roll, or Danish pastry (sweet roll) with coffee or tea (Continental breakfast) or the whole works: eggs (served with toast), sausages, pancakes (coated with maple syrup) or waffles in assorted flavours.

Brunch is generally eaten on lazy Sundays any time between 11am and 3pm. **Lunch**, from 11am to 2.30pm, can be anything from a gourmet affair served in luxurious surroundings (coat and tie, please) to a hurried hot dog, hamburger or *knish* (cheese-filled dumpling) washed down with an icy cola bought from a sidewalk vendor. **Dinner** is the serious big meal, served from as early as 5.30 until 10.30pm, often preceded by cocktails and accompanied by wine.

Where to Eat

It depends whether you have a craving for linguini with clam sauce, stuffed cabbage, canard à l'orange, Sauerbraten with potato pancakes, dim sum, paella, tempura or tacos – every kind of food is available here. If you're particularly fond of hot and spicy food, look for all snacks, appetizers or entrées marked 'Cajun style'.

In most parts of Manhattan you will find great restaurants (see pp.73-80). In the midtown area the best selection is in and around the Theater District between West 42nd and 55th Sts and on the East Side between Madison and Second Avenues. Further south, head for Greenwich Village, Chelsea, SoHo or one of the neighbourhoods of lower Manhattan – TriBeCa, Little Italy, Chinatown – or you can also try the World Financial Center or the World Trade Center.

At the Carnegie Deli, try the pastrami on rye, or bagel, lox and creamed cheese – or any other delicious combination!

Coffee shops as well as self-service cafeterias, found all over town, offer breakfast specials, hamburgers, French fries, soups, sandwiches, a variety of simple dishes and pastries. Alcohol is not usually sold in these establishments.

Delis are known for the gargantuan sandwiches they prepare with all kinds of bread and garnish with half-sour or dill pickles and coleslaw; other specialities include salads and hearty soups such as the refreshing cold borscht or the mushroom-barley soup. Some delicatessens are kosher.

Ethnic restaurants may be Greek, Italian, Japanese, Chinese, Spanish, Mexican, Indian, Middle Eastern, German, Russian, Scandinavian and so on: there's something to suit every imaginable taste. Some of the best Chinese and Italian restaurants are located in Chinatown and Little Italy, while Japanese restaurants tend to be in Midtown, where Thai cuisine is also making its mark. If German food takes your fancy, head up to East 86th Street in Yorkville between Lexington and First Avenues. The Indian subcontinent has cornered the strip of Lexington Ave north of Gramercy Park, and Middle Eastern restaurants are found on Atlantic Avenue in Brooklyn or – along with popular Greek, French, Spanish and Filipino cuisine – on Eighth Avenue between W 37th and 53rd Streets.

Fast-food outlets abound, as do pizzerias serving a great variety of enormous pizzas – you can also buy them by the slice for a quick snack.

Sidewalk **cafés** serve full meals, as well as sandwiches, quiches and crêpes. Some of the most pleasant are protected from the elements in the pedestrian areas, or atriums, of malls and skyscrapers such as the Citicorp Center.

Take-outs are either small kitchens or Korean fruit- and vegetable stands where you can order a meal, sandwich and salads as well as assorted groceries and soft drinks to take out and eat somewhere else.

Most New York restaurants charge more for dinner than for a comparable lunch. You can order a salad on its own if you like, but sometimes there is a minimum charge. Always ask about the 'special' (dish of the day). In all unpretentious places you pay the cashier on your way out, after leaving the usual tip on the table.

What to Eat

Sandwiches: they are made from white, rye, wholewheat, pumpernickel or pitta bread, rolls or even bagels (doughnut-shaped roll). Classic fillings include chicken, tuna and egg salads; lox (smoked salmon) with cream cheese, a delicious Jewish speciality served on a bagel; and chopped liver or pastrami, also of Jewish descent. You will also find club sandwiches, made up of three **111**

slices of toast garnished with lettuce, tomato, bacon, sometimes cheese; the hot dog, the all-beef New York variety usually served with sauerkraut or fried onions and mustard; and not forgetting hamburgers.

Soups: more and more small restaurants include a variety of soups on their menus. Chile con carne, that great Tex-Mex classic, is a substantial stew of kidney beans, ground beef, onions and tomatoes. It's served in a bowl.

Salads: many restaurants feature an appetizing self-service salad bar with a wide choice of dressing. The 'chef's salad', which may include chicken,

*T*ake a number and make your choice: New York's renowned delicatessens offer an awesome variety of mouth-watering dishes.

Tasty sandwiches are a good way to stave off any kind of hunger pang.

ham and cheese, is a meal in itself; raw spinach salad with mushrooms ranks as a great American original; Caesar salad has lettuce, croutons, Parmesan cheese and a raw egg in the dressing; coleslaw (cabbage salad) often appears with sandwiches; Waldorf salad is garnished with apples, walnuts and mayonnaise. You'll also find a wide variety of vegetable and fruit salads.

Meat: beef takes first place. In some steakhouses you pay a flat rate for a steak, French fries or a baked potato accompanied with sour cream, a self-service salad bar, and, in some cases, as much wine, beer or sangria as you like.

Other treats are 'spare ribs': pork ribs, marinated in a spicy sauce, baked or grilled; ham steak with a slice of pineapple – a speciality from the South –

and Long Island ducklings, famous for their flavour. Finally, the all-American holiday favourite, stuffed turkey, appears on menus all year round.

Fish and seafood: it's too often forgotten that New York is an ocean port abounding with fresh fish and seafood – witness the Fulton Fish Market (see p. 45). If you like shellfish, make the most of your stay here. The Long Island Blue Point oysters, subject to strict inspection, are a real delicacy. **113**

Clams and oysters on the half-shell come with chili and horseradish sauces and small crackers. As a special treat, oysters Rockefeller, filled with spinach, sprinkled with breadcrumbs and browned under a grill, are an unexpected but successful combination.

For a nice change from the perennial shrimp cocktail, try soft-shell crabs (in spring and summer). You can eat almost every morsel of these crabs, caught after they've cast their shells. Scallops, lobster and Nova Scotia salmon are special treats, and fish is good, too, usually grilled or deep-fried in batter.

Desserts: ice-cream comes in a wonderful variety of flavours. Cheesecake and apple pie, topped with a scoop of ice cream (à la mode) or whipped cream, are excellent, while pumpkin pie is a Thanksgiving Day tradition. Rice pudding and Jello (jelly) are coffee-shop staples. In most places you can also ask for fresh fruit or a fruit salad, which is sometimes offered as a first course.

Drinks: soft drinks are very popular, with cola drinks leading the market, but iced water is served with every meal, on request. Beer, served ice cold, falls into the lager category, but you can often find pale or brown ale and many foreign beers, either manufactured under licence or imported.

New York State produces decent **wines**; Californian ones are even better. French and Italian wines also appear on menus at reasonable prices.

In recent years wine has become a popular aperitif and spirits have gone somewhat out of fashion, but not the **cocktail** hour! Dry martinis (gin and a minimum of dry vermouth) are very potent. The best Bourbon whiskey comes from Kentucky, distilled from corn; some blends use rye. The Manhattan cocktail combines a drop of Bourbon with sweet vermouth and a maraschino cherry; an Old Fashioned comes on the rocks with a dash of bitters, sugar and a slice of orange, topped with a shot of soda water. Many bars have a late-afternoon 'happy hour'.

BLUEPRINT
for a
Perfect Trip

An A–Z Summary of Practical Information

> Certain items of information in this section will already be familiar to residents of the United States, but have been included for visitors from overseas.

A

ACCOMMODATIONS (See also YOUTH HOSTELS on p.139 and the list of RECOMMENDED HOTELS starting on p.66)

The New York Convention & Visitors Bureau (see TOURIST INFORMATION OFFICES on p.135) can give you an up-to-date list of **hotels**. You should book a room in advance if possible; the city can be very crowded during convention and holiday periods. Have your reservation confirmed before leaving for New York and bring the letter of confirmation with you. Rates do not include a tax of 19¼ percent (14¼ percent if the room rate is less than $100), plus a $2 per day occupancy tax. A few hotels and 'suite' hotels provide a Continental or buffet breakfast, but this is the exception, not the rule. Normally, unless you are on a prepaid tour, no meals will be included. At many hotels children can sleep in their parents' room at no extra charge.

In addition to the youth hostel, there are a number of residences run by the Young Men's (and Women's) Christian Association and the Young Men's Hebrew Association – the YMCA, YWCA and YMHA, commonly known as **Ys**. All the Ys have pools and exercise facilities and hotel taxes are not charged for stays at the AYH or Ys. You don't have to belong to any special organization or faith to stay in the Ys, but it's better to reserve a room by writing to the Resident Director. Three of the best Ys, open to both men and women, are:

Vanderbilt YMCA, 224 East 47th Street, New York, NY 10017; tel. 755-2410

West Side YMCA, 5 West 63rd Street, New York, NY 10023; tel. 787-4400

De Hirsch Residence (of the YMHA), 1395 Lexington Avenue at 92nd Street, New York, NY 10128; tel. 415-5650

AIRPORTS

New York is served by three major airports – **John F Kennedy International** (JFK) mainly for international flights, **LaGuardia** (LGA) and **Newark International** (EWR), mainly for domestic flights. There are half a dozen separate terminals at JFK, for individual airlines and groups of airlines.

Arriving from abroad, you must first present your passport and immigration card to an immigration official. He or she will attach a temporary residence visa to your passport which must be given back when you leave the country. After you've collected your luggage and gone through customs, hand the customs form over at the exit. There is a $1.50 charge for baggage carts that must be paid into a machine that makes change for dollar bills only. Carry cash for this purpose, as the money exchange facilities are outside the customs area.

The arrival scene at airports serving New York City is fairly chaotic. The simplest way of getting to your address in town is also the most expensive – the taxi (see TRANSPORT on p.136). Often you can arrange with a fellow passenger to share a cab and split the fare. Fares (subject to inflationary changes) from JFK and Newark are around $35 in normal traffic, and $20 from LaGuardia. Individuals who approach travellers inside the terminals offering a taxi service are unlicensed operators and best avoided. Transportation desks inside the terminals offer tickets for various services, including shared private cars and shared minibuses that are cheaper than taxis.

Gray Line Shuttle buses running every 30 minutes deliver to any address between 23rd and 63rd Streets for $15 from Newark and LaGuardia, $16 from JFK (tickets sold at the transportation desk).

Inter-airport bus and helicopter connections exist between Kennedy and both LaGuardia and Newark.

For detailed recorded information on transport to and from the airports, call the Port Authority's toll-free number: **1-800-AIR-RIDE**. **117**

Kennedy Airport. Carey Transportation runs express coaches from all airport terminals to midtown Manhattan. Buses leave every 30 minutes from 6am to midnight for the Carey ticket office at 125 Park Avenue between East 41st and 42nd Streets (opposite Grand Central Terminal) and continue to the Air TransCenter at Port Authority Bus Terminal (Eighth Avenue at West 42nd Street) and, for an extra $1.50, on to the midtown NY Hilton, Sheraton City Squire, Holiday Inn Crowne Plaza and Marriot Marquis hotels. The 15-mile (24km) trip from JFK takes from 45 to 75 minutes.

A regular 20-minute helicopter service (New York Helicopter) links JFK (TWA International Terminal) with the heliport on East River at East 34th Street for $65.

The cheapest means of transport (for the price of a token) is the subway. Catch the free shuttle bus marked 'Long Term Parking' to the parking lot adjoining the Howard Beach subway station. There, take the A train down Central Park West and 8th Avenue to Times Square (where a shuttle connects with the East Side) and on to Greenwich Village, the World Trade Center and Lower Manhattan.

LaGuardia Airport. Carey coaches also serve LaGuardia, leaving every 20 minutes for the same midtown addresses as the JFK buses. The 6-mile (10km) ride takes 45 minutes.

Quick Trip LaGuardia Express buses connect the airport to the 21st Street/Queensbridge subway station, where you can take the Q or B train to midtown.

A Delta Airlines Water Shuttle operates from LaGuardia's Marine Air Terminal down the East River to East 34th Street and Pier 11, just south of Wall Street ($20 one way, $30 round trip). For the schedule, ring 1-800-54-FERRY (toll-free).

Newark Airport. New Jersey Transit buses leave every 15 to 30 minutes from all airport terminals for the Port Authority Bus Terminal (Manhattan). The 16-mile (26km) trip takes 30 to 45 minutes.

Olympia Trail Airport Express also runs scheduled airport express buses. These leave the terminals every 20 to 30 minutes for midtown Manhattan at West 34th Street (near Penn Station) and Park Avenue at East 41st Street (near Grand Central Terminal), as well as for 1

World Trade Center (near the West Street entrance). The midtown trip takes from 35 to 65 minutes, the downtown one 20 to 45.

B

BICYCLE RENTAL/HIRE (See also MONEY MATTERS on p.128)

A list of rental agencies can be found in the Yellow Pages of the telephone directory under 'Bicycles: Dealers, Repairers & Rental'. Bikes can be rented in Central Park at the Loeb Boathouse.

C

CAR RENTAL/HIRE
(See also DRIVING on p.123 and MONEY MATTERS on p.128)

It's cheaper to rent a car at the airport or outside of Manhattan (you'll find agencies listed in the Yellow Pages under 'Automobile Renting & Leasing'). Prices are competitive, so it's worth shopping around. If you want to be sure of obtaining a particular model at the airport, make arrangements through an international agency before leaving home.

Most rental firms propose special weekend and unlimited-mileage rates; some offer rent-it-here, leave-it-there deals. It's often a good idea to reserve a week in advance for weekend rentals, especially from mid-May to mid-September.

Agencies generally prefer credit card transactions. The minimum age for renting a car is normally 21. Many agencies require an International Driving Permit if the renter's national licence is in a language other than English. Anyway, an IDP (or your driving licence accompanied by a translation) is highly recommended in case of an encounter with a local policeman.

CLIMATE and CLOTHING
New York is famous for hot, humid summers and cold winters. In spring and autumn there are glorious, clear, sunny days. The most pleasant times to visit are from mid-April to mid-June and mid-Sep- **119**

tember to early November. However, the city does make its own indoor climate, with extensive – many would say excessive – air conditioning in summer and heating in winter. There are about 3.5 inches (9cm) of rain a month.

Monthly average maximum and minimum daytime temperatures:

	J	F	M	A	M	J	J	A	S	O	N	D
max °F	39	40	48	61	71	81	85	83	77	67	54	41
min °F	26	27	34	44	53	63	68	66	60	51	41	30
max °C	7	4	9	16	22	27	29	28	25	19	12	5
min °C	3	3	1	7	12	17	20	19	15	10	5	1

Clothing. In New York you have to cope with extremes of temperature between winter and summer, but also between outdoors and indoors. Most stores overheat in winter and overcool in summer. In winter, don't forget your heavy coat, boots, warm hat and gloves.

In summer wear your lightest clothes, in natural fibres if possible. The air is so humid and sticky that you'll need several changes of clothing. Bring along a raincoat: you may be caught in a downpour.

COMMUNICATIONS (See also OPENING HOURS on p.130 and TIME DIFFERENCES on p.135)

Post Offices. The US Post Office only deals with mail. Branches are generally open weekdays from 8am to 5pm and on Saturday from 9am to 1pm. New York's General Post Office, 421 Eighth Avenue, New York, NY 10001, stays open 24 hours. You can also buy stamps at the reception desk in your hotel, in many grocery stores, or from stamp machines, though these may cost more than at the post office. Almost every street has its standard blue mailbox.

You can have mail sent to you c/o General Delivery (poste restante) to the General Post Office, or c/o American Express (without charge if you hold their credit card or traveller's cheque); envelopes should be marked 'Client's Mail'. Mail should be collected within 90 days; take your passport along for identification.

Telephones. Directions for use are on the instrument. Telephone
120 rates are listed and explained in the front of the White Pages of the

telephone directory. Also included is information on person-to-person (personal) calls, collect (reverse-charge) calls, conference, station-to-station and credit card calls. All numbers with an 800 prefix are toll-free. For long-distance calls in the US precede the area code with the number 1; precede international calls with 01.

New York has two area codes: **212** for Manhattan, **718** for Bronx, Queens, Brooklyn and Staten Island. For example, if you are in Manhattan and want to telephone a subscriber in Queens, such as one of the airports, dial 1-718 + subscriber's number.

Local calls cost 25 cents for the first three minutes, after which the operator will tell you to add more money. If you need assistance for an international call, dial 0 and ask for an overseas operator.

Some useful numbers:

Directory Assistance: 411

Parks (special events, usually free): 360-1333

Time: 967-1616

Weather: 976-1212

Emergency police or medical help: 911

Telegrams, Telex, Fax. American telegraph companies are privately run. The main companies, such as RCA and Western Union (Western Union International for overseas), are listed in the Yellow Pages directory under 'Telegraph Companies'. Cablegrams (international telegrams) and telexes may be sent from these offices or telephoned, expensively, from your hotel room and from public phones if you have an internationally accepted credit card. Virtually all hotels and many stationery stores have a fax service.

COMPLAINTS

If you feel you have reason to complain about retail stores or business practices, you should contact the **New York City Department of Consumer Affairs**: 42 Broadway, New York, NY 10013; tel. 487-8398 or 487-4444. To complain about taxi drivers or fares, see Transport on p.136.

CRIME (See also EMERGENCIES on p.125 and POLICE on p.133)

It's true that New York City's crime rate is high, theft is common, and tourists are always easy targets for robbery. However, by taking a few simple precautions, you can reduce the risk:

● always lock your hotel room door

● deposit valuables in the hotel safe

● never carry large amounts of cash; wear a minimum of jewellery

● carry as much money as possible in the form of traveller's cheques, and keep a record of these (and your passport) separate from the cheques

● never leave valuables (bags, etc.) unattended or behind your back even for a few seconds.

If you *are* robbed, don't play the hero – hand over what you have. Then report it to the police immediately (tel. 374-5000 or 911 for emergencies): your insurance company will need to see a copy of the police report (as may your consulate if your passport is stolen). For stolen or lost traveller's cheques and credit cards, report the matter at once to the issuer so that payments can be stopped immediately.

CUSTOMS and ENTRY FORMALITIES
(See also AIRPORTS on p.117)

Canadians only need provide evidence of their nationality. UK citizens no longer need a visa for stays of less than 90 days, but only a valid 10-year passport and a return airline ticket. The airline will issue a visa waiver form. Citizens of the Republic of Ireland, Australia, New Zealand and South Africa need a visa – check with your local US consulate or embassy and allow three weeks for delivery.

Duty-free allowance. You will be asked to complete a customs declaration form before you arrive in the US. Restrictions are as follows, into: **USA**: 200 cigarettes or 50 cigars or 2kg tobacco, 1l of wine or spirits; **Australia**: 250 cigarettes or 250g tobacco, 1l alcohol; **Canada**: 200 cigarettes and 50 cigars and 400g tobacco, 1.1l wine or spirits or 8.5l beer; **New Zealand**: 200 cigarettes or 50 cigars or 250g tobacco, 4.5l wine or beer and 1.1l spirits; **Republic of Ire-**

land: 200 cigarettes or 50 cigars or 250g tobacco, 2l wine or 1l spirits; **South Africa**: 400 cigarettes and 50 cigars and 250g tobacco, 2l wine and 1l spirits; **UK**: 200 cigarettes or 50 cigars or 250g tobacco, 2l wine or 1l spirits.

A non-resident may claim, free of duty and taxes, articles up to $100 in value for use as gifts for other persons. The exemption is valid only if the gifts accompany you, you stay 72 hours or more and have not claimed this exemption within the preceding six months. Up to 100 cigars may be included within this gift exemption (Cuban cigars, however, are forbidden and may be confiscated).

Arriving and departing passengers must report any money or cheques etc. exceeding a total of $10,000.

D

DRIVING (See also CAR RENTAL/HIRE on p.119)

Driving conditions. Visitors arriving by car would do well to leave it parked in a garage and use local transport, as traffic and scarce parking space make driving a chore. If you must drive, remember certain rules: the speed limit is 30mph (50kph) unless otherwise indicated; you may not use your horn in town; the use of seat belts is mandatory; the speed limit on most highways is 55mph (90kph) and strictly enforced; and, of course, visitors from the UK must remember to drive on the right. Before leaving home, determine whether your own insurance will cover you when driving a rented car. If it does, you need not take the car rental insurance.

Parking. The city has a considerable number of car parks (listed in the Yellow Pages under 'Parking Stations & Garages'), useful since it's next to impossible to find a place to park on the street. If you happen to find one, obey posted parking regulations, which may include parking only on one side of the street on alternate days. Never park next to a fire hydrant and don't leave your car over the time limit, or it may be towed away to a police parking lot – a costly proposition!

On Manhattan there are 16 bridges; tolls are charged on some, and are also payable for the underwater tunnels serving Manhattan. **123**

Gas (petrol). Service stations are few and far between in the city. They are often open in the evening and on Sundays.

Breakdowns and insurance. The Automobile Club of New York (ACNY), a branch of the American Automobile Association (AAA), will help members, as well as foreign visitors affiliated with other recognized automobile associations. In case of breakdown or for other problems along the way, call their Emergency Road Service on 757-3356; or wait until a state police patrol car comes along.

ACNY: 1881 Broadway, New York, NY 10019; tel. 586-1166.

AAA: 1415 Kellum Place, Garden City, New York, NY 11530; tel. 586-1166. The AAA offers information on travelling in the US and short-term insurance (1-12 months); AAA World Wide Travel: 1000 AAA Drive, Heathrow, FL 32746-5063; tel. 1-407-444-4300.

Road signs. Foreign visitors may be unfamiliar with those signs:

Detour	Diversion
Divided highway	Dual carriageway
No passing	No overtaking
Railroad crossing	Level crossing
Roadway	Carriageway
Traffic circle	Roundabout
Yield	Give way

Distance

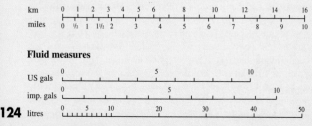

Fluid measures

ELECTRIC CURRENT

110-volt 60-cycle AC is standard throughout the US. Plugs are the flat, two-pronged variety. Foreign visitors without dual-voltage appliances will need a transformer and adaptor plug for their electric razors, hair dryers and travel irons.

EMBASSIES and CONSULATES

Australia: 630 Fifth Avenue; tel. 245-4000

Canada: 1251 Avenue of the Americas; tel. 768-2400

Republic of Ireland: 515 Madison Avenue; tel. 319-2555

New Zealand: Washington, DC; tel. 1-202-328-4880

South Africa: 333 East 38th Street; tel. 213-4880

United Kingdom: 845 Third Avenue; tel. 745-0202

EMERGENCIES (See also MEDICAL CARE on p.127 and POLICE on p.133)

All-purpose emergency number: **911**

Dentist Emergency Service: **679-3966**

Doctors On Call: **1-718-238-2100**

If you dial **0**, the telephone operator will connect you with the emergency services.

GAY and LESBIAN TRAVELLERS

Gay and Lesbian Switchboard: 777-1800. For gay events and news, the *New York Native* is published weekly. *Stonewall News*, *HX*, *Next*, and *The Advocate* are other publications geared to a gay audience. **125**

GUIDES and TOURS

The best way to get started in New York is to take a bus tour. There are many operators and some may pick up near your hotel. Most start in or near Times Square. Numerous agencies offer organized tours and special excursions (walking tours, helicopter, nightclub rounds, historical tours, etc.). Individual guides are also available.

For some amusingly off-beat tours, try Sidewalks of New York (tel. 517-0201) or Big Onion Walking Tours (tel. 439-1090). For other possibilities, check the Friday and Sunday *New York Times* or contact the New York Convention & Visitors Bureau (see p.135).

L

LANGUAGE

Most English-speaking foreigners are familiar with American words and phrases, but here are a few that may cause confusion:

US	British
bathroom	toilet (private)
bill	note (money)
check	bill
first floor/2nd floor	ground floor/first floor
pavement	road surface
restroom	toilet (public)
sidewalk	pavement
underpass	subway

LAUNDRY and DRY CLEANING

All first-class hotels have efficient same-day service and some even provide drying lines in the bathroom.

You can find self-service laundries where coin-operated washing machines and dryers are available. Look under 'Laundries – Self-Service' in the Manhattan Yellow Pages or ask the hotel receptionist.

Combination dry cleaners and laundries abound in residential areas a few blocks from midtown hotel zones. They usually provide one-day service for an extra charge. They are also listed in the directory's Yellow Pages under 'Cleaners & Dryers'. Self-service laundromats where you pay according to weight are also available.

LOST PROPERTY

Each transport system maintains its own lost property office. Here are two useful numbers:

New York City Transit Authority (NYCTA) Lost Property Office (subway network and bus system): tel. 1-718-625-6200.

NYC Taxi & Limousine Commission Lost Property: tel. (212) 840-4734/4735/4736.

M

MEDIA

Radio and Television. You'll almost certainly have a radio and television in your hotel room, with a vast choice of programmes, especially with cable TV. New York has about 60 AM-FM radio stations.

All television stations transmit round the clock. Channels 13, 21 and 25, the Public Broadcasting Service, have no commercials. The major news broadcasts can be watched at 5.30am on Channels 4 and 7, at 6.30am on Channel 2, and at 6.30pm on all channels.

Newspapers and magazines. The city's major newspapers are the *Daily News*, *New York Times* and *New York Post*. The *Sunday New York Times* includes a comprehensive arts and leisure section and the Friday paper has a useful section listing weekend events. The weekly publications – *The New Yorker*, *New York Magazine* and *The Village Voice* – are helpful for finding out what's going on in the city.

For the best selection of foreign newspapers and magazines, go to Hotalings at 142 West 42nd Street, the news-stand in the concourse below the RCA-General Electric Building at Rockefeller Center or the news-stands in the lobbies of larger hotels.

MEDICAL CARE (See also Emergencies on p.125)

Arrangements for health and accident insurance during your trip should be made before your visit through your travel agency or an insurance company, or ask at your local Social Security office.

Except in an emergency, foreign visitors should call their consulate for a list of doctors in New York City. In any emergency, local telephone operators are an excellent source of advice.

Drugstores. There is usually a pharmacy at the rear of a drugstore. Prescriptions written by foreign doctors will rarely be filled, and the brand names of many drugs will be different in the US. It is best to bring with you any medicines you require regularly. If you need special drugs, you will have to get a prescription by a local doctor. In central Manhattan, **Kaufman's Pharmacy**, 557 Lexington Avenue at East 50th St, tel. 755-2266, is open 24 hours, seven days a week.

MONEY MATTERS

Currency. The dollar is divided into 100 cents. The coins are as follows: 1¢ (penny), 5¢ (nickel), 10¢ (dime), 25¢ (quarter), 50¢ (half-dollar; rare) and $1 (rare). Banknotes of $1, $5, $10, $20, $50 and $100 are common; higher denominations also exist. All denominations are the same size and colour, so be sure to double-check your cash before you spend it. For currency restrictions, see Customs and Entry Formalities on p.122.

Exchange facilities. Most banks are open weekdays from 9am to 3pm (often till 6pm on Thursdays). Currency exchange offices at the airport remain open at the weekend. All branches of the Chemical Bank and Bank Leumi, many branches of Citibank and major offices of other banks now change foreign currency and foreign traveller's cheques. Private exchange bureaus which stay open longer hours have sprung up in tourist areas – look under 'Foreign Money Brokers' in the Yellow Pages. You may be able to change money at your hotel, though you probably won't get the bank rate. A supply of $1 banknotes (for taxis, toll bridges, tipping, etc.) is always useful.

Credit cards. The major cards are accepted as cash almost everywhere. When paying for goods or services, including hotel and restaurant bills, you will be asked: 'Cash or charge?', meaning you have the choice of paying either in cash or 'plastic money'.

Traveller's cheques. Visitors from abroad will find traveller's cheques drawn on American banks far easier to deal with. Cash only small amounts at a time, and keep the balance in the hotel safe if possible. Keep your receipt and a list of the serial numbers of the cheque in a separate place to facilitate a refund in case of loss or theft.

Sales tax. Expect to have state and city taxes – a total of 8¼ percent – added to the marked-up price of all goods purchased in New York City, including meals.

PLANNING YOUR BUDGET

To give you an idea of what to expect, here's a list of average prices in US dollars. They can only be approximate, however, as inflation creeps up relentlessly.

Airport transfer. Taxi (excluding tolls and tip) from JFK to Manhattan about $35, from LaGuardia $20, from Newark International $40. Bus from JFK to Grand Central Terminal or Port Authority Bus Terminal (Air TransCenter) $11, from LaGuardia $8.50, from Newark International to Port Authority or World Trade Center $7.

Babysitters. $10-12.50 per hour (four hours min.) for one child, plus transport ($4.50 up to midnight, $7 after midnight).

Bicycle rental/hire. $4-7 per hour (depending on whether 3- or 10-speed), $18-27 for full day, deposit $20.

Buses. $1.25 a trip, including transfer on certain lines (but you must ask for it when you pay). Exact change or token is required.

Car rental/hire. Prices vary enormously, depending on the season and the firm. The cheaper weekly rates apply only when a car is reserved a week in advance. Cars are expensive to rent in Manhattan.

Cigarettes (packet of 20). $2.25 and up, plus tax.

Entertainment. Movies $7.50. Theatre $35-70 on Broadway, $10-50 Off-Broadway. Ballet, concerts $15-50. Museums $5-8, skyscrapers $4, nightclubs $10-50.

Film/video cassette. 24-exposure print film $4-5.50; 36-exposure print film $5-$7. 24-exposure slide film $5.50-$; 36-exposure slide film $7.50-12. Blank VHS-120 video tapes $3, VHS-160 video tapes $5 (NB: American VHS tapes do not function on European VCRs).

Guided tours. City bus tour $15. Circle Line boat trip around Manhattan $18, children under 12 $9. Walking tour of New York $10-15 per person. Atlantic City day trip $20-25. Horse-drawn carriage tour of Central Park $34 for 20 minutes.

Helicopter tours. $47-$119 per person, depending on length and duration of flight, plus $5 fee for booking ticket.

Hotels (double occupancy per night), tax not included. Budget category up to $100, moderate $100-200, luxury $200-700.

Restaurants (tax not included). Breakfast $5 and up, lunch in coffee shop $7 and up, in restaurant $18 and up, dinner $25 and up, glass of wine $3 and up, bottle of wine $18 and up, glass of beer $2.50 and up, whisky $4.50 and up, soft drink $1.50 and up, coffee $1 and up.

Subway. Token $1.25.

Taxis. Meter starts at $1.50; there's a charge of 25 cents per one-fifth of a mile of travel; 20 cents per minute waiting time and a night surcharge of 50 cents (8pm-6am).

YMCA-YMHA. Double room $48-56, single room $30-45; New York International AYH-Hostel, about $20 per person for International Youth Hostel members, additional $3 for others.

OPENING HOURS

Banks. 9am-3pm, sometimes 8am-6pm Mon-Fri; most open 9am-noon/2pm Saturday.

Sights and museums. See p.81 for New York's museum highlights. NB: Most art museums are closed on Mondays.

Abigail Adams Smith Museum: 421 E 61st St, tel. 838-6878. Open Mon-Fri noon to 4pm, Sun 1-5pm. Closed in August.

American Craft Museum: In the EF Hutton tower at 40 W 53rd St, tel. 956-3535. Open Tues 10am-8pm; Wed-Sun 10am-5pm.

American Museum of Natural History: Central Park West at W 79th St, tel. 769-5100. Open Mon-Thurs 10am-5.45pm, Fri-Sat 10am-8.45pm.

Asia Society: 725 Park Ave at 70th St; tel. 288-6400. Open Tues-Sat llam-6pm; Thurs 11am-8pm; Sun noon-5pm.

The Brooklyn Museum: Eastern Parkway at Washington Ave (Brooklyn), tel. (718) 638-5000. Open Wed-Sun 10am-5pm. Take No. 2 or 3 express subway from Times Square. The trip to the nearest station (Eastern Parkway–Brooklyn Museum) takes half an hour.

The Children's Museum of Manhattan: 212 W 83rd St near Broadway, tel. 721-1234. Open Mon, Wed, Thurs 1.30-5.30pm, Fri, Sat, Sun 10am-5pm.

The Cloisters: Fort Tryon Park, tel. 923-3700. (This is a branch of the Metropolitan Museum of Art.) Open Tues-Sun 9.30am-4.45pm; March-Oct Tues-Sun 9.30am-5.15pm.

Cooper-Hewitt Museum: E 91st St at Fifth Ave, tel. 860-6898. Open Tues 10am-9pm; Wed-Sat 10am-5pm; Sun noon-5pm.

Empire State Building viewing floors: 350 Fifth Avenue. Open every day from 9.30am until 11.30pm.

Federal Hall National Memorial (at the junction of Wall & Nassau Sts): open weekdays 9am-5pm.

Fraunces Tavern Museum: 54 Pearl St, tel. 425-1778. Open weekdays 10am-4.45pm, Sat noon-4pm.

The Frick Collection: E 70th St at Fifth Ave, tel. 288-0700. Open Tues-Sat 10am-6pm; Sun 1-6pm. Children from 10 to 16 admitted if accompanied by an adult; no children under 10.

Gottesman Hall, New York Public Library: Fifth Ave at 42 St, tel. 869-8089. Free entry; closed Sundays and public holidays.

Grant's Tomb: W 122nd St. Open from Wed-Sun 9am-5pm.

Solomon R Guggenheim Museum: 1071 Fifth Ave at E 88th St, tel. 423-3500. Open 10am-8pm; closed Thursday. *SoHo branch*: at 575

Broadway. Open Sun, Mon, Wed 11am-6pm; Thurs, Fri and Sat till 8pm.

International Center of Photography: Fifth Ave at E 94th St, tel. 860-1777. Open Tues 11am-8pm; Wed-Sun 11am-6pm. *Midtown branch*: Ave of the Americas and W 43rd St; tel 768-4682. Same hours.

The Intrepid Sea-Air-Space Museum: Pier 86 at 112th Ave and W 46th St, tel. 245-0072. Open Wed-Sun, 10am-5pm.

The Jewish Museum: Fifth Ave at 92nd St, tel. 423-3200. Open Sun, Mon, Wed, Thurs 11am-5.45pm, Tues 11am-8pm.

Lincoln Center: tel. 875-5400. One-hour guided tours start from the concourse daily from 10am to 5pm.

The Metropolitan Mus. of Art: Fifth Ave at E 82nd St, tel. 535-7710. Open Sun, Tues, Wed, Thurs 9.30am-5.15pm; Fri, Sat 9.30am-8.45pm.

Morris-Jumel Mansion and gardens, Jumel Terrace and W 161st St, Harlem: open Wed-Sun 10am-4pm.

Museum of the City of New York: Fifth Ave at 103rd St, tel. 534-1672. Open Wed-Sat 10am-5pm; Sun 1-5pm. Open Tuesday for organized group tours only.

The Museum of Modern Art: W 53rd St between Fifth and Sixth Aves, tel. 708-9480. Open Sat-Wed 11am-6pm; Thurs-Fri 12am-8.30pm.

Museum of Television and Radio: 25 W 52nd St, tel. 621-6600. Open Tues, Wed, Fri-Sun noon-6pm; Thurs noon-8pm.

The National Museum of the American Indian, Smithsonian Institution; the Hispanic Society of America; and the American Numismatic Society: US Customs House, Bowling Green, tel. 283-2497. Open Tues-Sat 10am-5pm, Sun 1-5pm.

NBC at the RCA Building: a tour behind the scenes of the broadcasting studios starts at 30 Rockefeller Plaza (Mon-Sat 9.30 or 10am-4 or 4.30pm; children under six are not permitted).

The New Museum of Contemporary Art: 583 Broadway between Prince and Houston Sts, tel. 219-1355. Open Wed, Thurs and Sun noon-6pm; Fri, Sat, noon-8pm.

New York Stock Exchange: 20 Broad St, tel. 656-5168. Open during most of the Exchange's trading hours (weekdays 9.15am-4pm).

Pierpont Morgan Library: 29 E 36th St at Madison Av, tel. 685-0610. Open Tues-Sat 10.30am-5pm; Sun 1-5pm.

Radio City Music Hall: Rockefeller Center. Tours between 10.15am and 4.45pm, starting at 11.15am on Sundays, tel. 632-4041.

South Street Seaport Museum: East River at the foot of Fulton St, tel. 669-9400. Open Mon-Sun 10am-5pm. Same telephone for *Children's Center Museum*.

Whitney Museum of American Art: Madison Ave at E 75th St, tel. 570-3676. Open Wed, Fri-Sun 11am-6pm, Thurs 1-8pm, closed Mon-Thurs.

World Trade Center viewing floors: Chambers St, tel. 435-7377. Open 9.30am-9.30pm daily and to 11.30pm in summer.

Tourist Information Offices. Open 9am-6pm Mon-Fri; Sat, Sun 10am-6pm.

P

PHOTOGRAPHY and VIDEO

All popular brands of film and photographic equipment are available. Try to buy in discount stores where prices are much lower, but check the validity dates. Airport X-ray machines do not normally affect ordinary film, but ask for hand inspection of high-speed film. Protect any film in a lightweight insulating bag. Video tape is available for all types of camera. Pre-recorded tapes bought in the US do not function on European video players (and vice versa). Tapes can be converted, but at considerable expense.

POLICE (See also CRIME on p.121 and EMERGENCIES on p.125)

In an emergency, dial **911**. The New York police department is highly visible: on foot, horseback, motorbikes and in cars. You will also see them patrolling the subway. Guardian Angels patrol the subway and midtown streets, though they have no official power.

PUBLIC HOLIDAYS

In New York banks, many museums, federal offices and some stores are closed on the following holidays:

New Year's Day	1 January
Martin Luther King Day*	Third Monday in January
President's Day*	Third Monday in February
Memorial Day	Last Monday in May
Independence Day	4 July
Labor Day	First Monday in September
Columbus Day*	Second Monday in October
Veterans' Day*	11 November
Thanksgiving Day	Fourth Thursday in November
Christmas Day	25 December

* Partially or optionally observed.

R

RELIGION

The Yellow Pages of the telephone directory list the locations and phone numbers of places of worship for a great diversity of faiths reflecting New York's eclectic composition. Here's a cross-section for different denominations:

Roman Catholic: St Patrick's Cathedral, Fifth Avenue between East 50th and 51st Streets (opposite Rockefeller Center); tel. 753-2261.

Episcopalian: Cathedral Church of St John the Divine, Amsterdam Avenue at West 112th Street; tel. 316-7540.

Jewish: Temple Emanu-El, East 65th Street at Fifth Avenue; tel. 744-1400.

Methodist: Lexington United Methodist Church, 150 East 62nd Street; tel. 838-6915.

Muslim: Islamic Center of New York, East 96th Street between Second and Third Avenues; tel. 722-5234.

Presbyterian: Central Presbyterian Church, 593 Park Avenue; tel. 838-0808.

Zen Studies Society: 223 East 67th Street; tel. 861-3333.

TIME DIFFERENCES

The continental United States has four time zones; New York City is on Eastern Standard Time. In summer (between April and October) Daylight Saving Time is adopted and clocks move ahead one hour. The following chart shows the time in various cities in winter:

Los Angeles	**New York**	London	Sydney
9am	**noon**	5pm	4am
Sunday	**Sunday**	Sunday	Monday

Dates in the US are written as follows: month/day/year; for example: 1/6/99 means 6 January 1999.

TIPPING

Service is never included in a restaurant bill, but is sometimes added to it. The usual tip is 15 percent (work out an approximation by doubling the 8¼ percent tax marked on your bill). Cinema or theatre ushers and filling-station attendants are not tipped. In general, porters are tipped $1 per bag, cloakroom attendants and doormen who find you a taxi $1, taxi drivers and hairdressers 15 percent.

TOURIST INFORMATION OFFICES

The New York Convention & Visitors Bureau is a non-profit organization subsidized by the city's hotels and merchants. The multilingual staff will give you maps and leaflets about tourist attractions, a price list of major hotels (mainly those that support the Bureau) and any further information: 2 Columbus Circle, New York, NY 10019 (tel. 397-8222). Hours: weekdays 9am-6pm; Sat, Sun 10am-6pm. **135**

The Travelers' Aid Society has offices at airports, bus and train stations. New York City offices are at 1481 Broadway; tel. 944-0013.

The Automobile Club of New York (ACNY) offers helpful advice on motoring and public transport in the US. Call 757-2000.

For information prior to arrival in the US, contact the United States Travel and Tourism Administration in your own country.

TRANSPORT (See also AIRPORTS on p.117, CAR HIRE on p.119 DRIVING on p.123 and TRAVELLING TO NEW YORK on p.138)

Bus and subway maps are available free at the token booths at major subway stations, the information booths at Grand Central Terminal and Port Authority Bus Terminal and at the New York Convention & Visitors Bureau. For assistance, call New York City Transit Authority (1-718-330-1234). Children under 44 inches (1.10m) travel free.

Buses. All public buses are numbered and bear the prefix M. Most either follow the avenues (except Park Ave.) or run crosstown along the major two-way arteries. A number of buses follow a special pattern and it is advisable to learn about these from the free bus maps.

Bus stops are indicated by a signpost showing a red-and-white 'No standing' sign, a blue-and-white bus logo and the bus number. Avenue buses usually stop at every second or third block, crosstown buses at the corner of each avenue. Hail the drivers.

Enter by the front door and deposit a token (the same ones used on the subway and sold only at subway stations and some news-stands) or the exact change (no banknotes or pennies) in the box next to the driver. A free transfer ticket is available for bus routes that intersect or continue the route (ask for a 'transfer' when boarding).

Subway. It operates 24 hours a day. You can purchase tokens from the booth in each station. Some booths close at night, so buy a handful or '10-pack' of tokens. Avoid rush hours (6-9.30am and 4-7pm).

Once you have entered the subway, you may travel to any destination, changing trains as required. Unless you are sure that the train stops at your destination, catch a 'local' rather than an 'express'.

The subway is generally safe: over four million New Yorkers ride it daily. At night it's safer to take a taxi. Some useful numbers:

Long Island Railroad (rail service between Manhattan and Brooklyn, Queens, Nassau County and Suffolk County): 516-822-LIRR (from Long Island) and 718-217-LIRR (from New York City).

Metro-North Commuter Railroad (between Manhattan and counties to the north of New York, including southwest Connecticut): 1-800-Metro-Info (outside NYC) and 212-532-4900 (within NYC).

Taxis. All legal taxis are yellow and have meters. Unoccupied cabs have an illuminated light on the roof. Taxis may be found stationed outside Grand Central and Penn Stations and at major hotels, but they tend to cruise continually. The meter starts at $1.50 and increases by 25 cents every one-fifth of a mile (or 20 cents for waiting time). There is a 50-cent surcharge between 8pm and 6am. If your route comprises a toll tunnel or bridge, you must pay the toll. Taxi drivers don't have to change banknotes higher than $5. Give the driver a tip of at least 15 percent, more for special service.

To complain about a driver, note his or her name and number and contact the NYC Taxi and Limousine Commission (tel. 221-8294).

Trains. Amtrak offers USA Railpasses (flat-rate unlimited rail travel for a month or longer). Various package deals are also available for link-ups with car rental agencies, bus companies and hotel groups – even 'railsail' packages, connecting with Caribbean cruises.

If you are going to Boston, Philadelphia, Baltimore or Washington, you may prefer Amtrak's Metroliner Service, fast luxury trains with reserved seating in club cars or leg-rest coaches. To book a seat, call toll-free 1-800-523-8720 for the Metroliner Service, 582-6875 for all other Amtrak services. For reservations and information at other points nationwide, call 1-800-USA-RAIL (1-800-872-7245). Children under two travel free; from two to 11 half fare is charged.

There are three main stations: **Penn Station**, underneath Madison Square Garden, is the most important for long-distance travel and serves Long Island and New Jersey commuters. **Grand Central Station**, on East 42nd Street, has suburban and Connecticut lines. **PATH stations**, for trains to New Jersey, are located below the World Trade Center, at Christopher Street and along Avenue of the Americas. **137**

TRAVELLERS WITH DISABILITIES

Most New York streetcorners are graded for wheelchairs, which are available at all airports (book ahead through your airline) and in most museums.

Legislation has been introduced requiring new hotels to provide facilities for visitors with disabilities, and many older establishments now also comply. Check when booking. The Mayor's Office for People with Disabilities, 52 Chambers St, Room 206, New York, NY 10007; tel. 788-2830, can give further information.

TRAVELLING TO NEW YORK

From the United States and Canada

By Air. There is a daily service between New York and at least one city in every state of the union, Toronto and Montreal. Major cities are linked with New York by hourly non-stop flights during the day.

By Bus. The major cities in North America have regular bus connections with New York. The only requirement is that the destination be reached within 60 days of the ticket being purchased. You save about 10 percent on round-trip tickets. Greyhound Trailways Bus Lines offer flat-rate Rover passes for specified periods of unlimited travel.

By Rail. Amtrak trains link New York City with the rest of the country. They feature the USA Railpass for unlimited travel at a flat rate for given periods of time and offer package tours to New York which include hotel accommodations. The Montrealer runs from Montreal to New York, with excellent connections from other parts of Canada.

From the United Kingdom and the Republic of Ireland

By Air. Apart from the standard first-class and economy fares, the main types of fares available are the Super APEX, Special Economy and Standby. Senior discounts may be available. An 'Open Jaws' reduced fare can lower the price of the Apex even more, though it does require entry and departure from different 'gateway' cities.

From Australia and New Zealand

From Australia: There's a twice-weekly air service from Sydney to New York via Los Angeles. Package deals, excursion and APEX **138** fares are available.

From New Zealand: Scheduled flights leave daily for New York from Auckland via Los Angeles. Excursion fares allow intermediate stops. EPIC fares do not permit stopovers.

WEIGHTS and MEASURES (See also DRIVING on p.124)
There are some slight differences between British and American measures, for instance: 1 US gallon = 0.833 British Imp. gallon = 3.8 litres; 1 US quart = 0.833 British Imp. quart = 0.9 litres

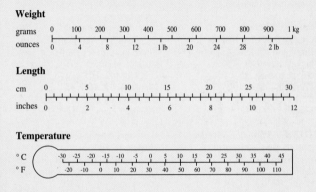

Weight

| grams | 0 | 100 | 200 | 300 | 400 | 500 | 600 | 700 | 800 | 900 | 1 kg |
| ounces | 0 | 4 | 8 | 12 | 1 lb | 20 | 24 | 28 | 2 lb |

Length

| cm | 0 | 5 | 10 | 15 | 20 | 25 | 30 |
| inches | 0 | 2 | 4 | 6 | 8 | 10 | 12 |

Temperature

| °C | -30 -25 -20 -15 -10 -5 0 5 10 15 20 25 30 35 40 45 |
| °F | -20 -10 0 10 20 30 40 50 60 70 80 90 100 110 |

WOMEN TRAVELLERS
Women travelling alone may wish to stay at a YWCA (see p.116). The Traveler's Aid Society, tel. 944-0013, can offer assistance.

YOUTH HOSTELS (See also ACCOMMODATIONS on p.116)
The New York International AYH-Hostel can be contacted at 891 Amsterdam Avenue, New York, NY 10025 (tel. 932-2300).

Index

Where there is more than one set of references, the one in **bold** refers to the main entry, the one in *italic* to a photograph.

Berlitz – pack the world in your pocket!

Africa
Algeria
Kenya
Morocco
South Africa
Tunisia

Asia, Middle East
China
Egypt
Hong Kong
India
Indonesia
Japan
Jerusalem
Malaysia
Singapore
Sri Lanka
Taiwan
Thailand

Australasia
Australia
New Zealand
Sydney

Austria, Switzerland
Austrian Tyrol
Switzerland
Vienna

**Belgium,
The Netherlands**
Amsterdam
Brussels

British Isles
Channel Islands
Dublin
Ireland
London
Scotland

**Caribbean, Latin
America**
Bahamas
Bermuda
Cancún and Cozumel
Caribbean
French West Indies
Jamaica
Mexico

Mexico City/Acapulco
Puerto Rico
Rio de Janeiro
Southern Caribbean
Virgin Islands

**Central and
Eastern Europe**
Budapest
Hungary
Moscow and
St Petersburg
Prague

France
Brittany
Châteaux of the Loire
Côte d'Azur
Dordogne
Euro Disney Resort
France
Normandy
Paris
Provence

Germany
Berlin
Munich
Rhine Valley

**Greece, Cyprus
and Turkey**
Athens
Corfu
Crete
Cyprus
Greek Islands
Istanbul
Rhodes
Turkey

Italy and Malta
Florence
Italy
Malta
Naples
Rome
Sicily
Venice

North America
Alaska Cruise Guide

Boston
California
Canada
Florida
Greater Miami
Hawaii
Los Angeles
Montreal
New Orleans
New York
San Francisco
Toronto
USA
Walt Disney World
and Orlando
Washington

Portugal
Algarve
Lisbon
Madeira

Scandinavia
Copenhagen
Helsinki
Oslo and Bergen
Stockholm
Sweden

Spain
Barcelona
Canary Islands
Costa Blanca
Costa Brava
Costa del Sol
Costa Dorada and
Barcelona
Costa Dorada and
Tarragona
Ibiza and Formentera
Madrid
Mallorca and Menorca
Seville

IN PREPARATION
Disneyland and the
Theme Parks of South-
ern California
Milan and the Italian
Lakes